MW01601687

The
Ultimate Guide to
Portable
Sawmills

Publisher
Norwood Sawmills
(Norwood Industries Inc.)

Editor
Ashlynne Dale

Contributors
Dave Boyt
Ashlynne Dale
Tina Lorenz

Book Design
Integra Design Studio Inc.

Illustrations
Andy Mora

Your **Biggest Sawmilling Questions Answered!**

✓ **Game Changing Secrets For Sawmilling Success**
✓ **Milling For Money**
✓ **7 Essentials for Choosing The Right Sawmill**
✓ **Cutting – Drying – Grading**
✓ **Plus PLANS – Build Your World!**

Richard E. Primeau

"The moment I got my hands on my Norwood Portable Sawmill ... the creativity began!! ... Never before had I ever built a wooden structure!! ... A portable sawmill made it so easy and saved me so much money, I just kept on going and going until I ended up with this 15x20 foot Pine Shed!!

I'm building another 8x15 pine garage for my Kubota tractor in the spring!! ... Can't wait to smell the fresh pine scent from the logs as my Norwood Sawmill planks my lumber!! ... I'm hooked!!"

— Richard Primeau

Issued in print and electronic formats.
ISBN: 978-0-9961369-0-7 (print)
ISBN: 978-0-9961369-1-4 (pdf)

Publisher
Norwood Sawmills (Norwood Industries Inc.)

Editor
Ashlynne Dale

Contributors
Dave Boyt
Ashlynne Dale
Tina Lorenz

Book Design
Integra Design Studio Inc.

Illustrations
Andy Mora

Printed in Canada

Norwood Sawmills

U.S.A.: 730 Young Street, Suite 900
Tonawanda, NY 14150

Canada: 2267 15/16 Side Road East
Oro-Medonte, ON L0L 1T0

www.NorwoodSawmills.com

Sawyers the world over share remarkable and admirable qualities —
integrity, resourcefulness, authenticity, self-reliance, honor.

This book is dedicated to sawyers —
hardworking people who understand what it means
to put in an honest day's work,
to strive for a better life for their families,
to dream big and have the courage to back it up with action.

TABLE OF CONTENTS

The Ultimate Guide to Portable Sawmills

INTRODUCTION

How One Man's Dream Became the First Affordable Portable Sawmill

Welcome to the wonderful world of portable sawmills!

Before you get started digging into the vast array of portable sawmill tips and strategies you'll find in these pages, let's take a look at how the dream of building a cozy cabin in the woods led to a brilliant solution that now transforms lives worldwide.

Admittedly, the story is near and dear to our collective hearts here at Norwood Sawmills.

Because not only did it turn one man's dream into a legacy…it has literally become the lifeblood of a thriving industry we're proud to be a part of.

It all began more than 20 years ago when Norwood founder Peter Dale decided it was time to turn his heart's desire for a cabin in the woods into a reality.

But there was a problem, and it was a big one.

Between the cost of lumber and portable sawmill prices, there was no way this family man could manage it on his modest income.

He quickly realized there was only one thing to do: Build his own band sawmill.

And it had to be done right. That meant, in addition to being affordable, it had to be strong, reliable, and accurate.

Peter Dale wasn't one to take shortcuts. So for two solid years, he designed, tested, and overcame a multitude of challenges. He never gave up.

You might say he was kind of a genius when it came to portable sawmills!

In fact, after starting from scratch with nothing more than grit and determination, a revolutionary breakthrough in portable sawmilling was born…

The First Norwood LumberMate

Norwood founder, Peter Dale, operating an original LumberMate

Peter Dale invented novel designs, adopted innovative technology, and applied simple yet effective mechanical concepts in creative ways.

And that is exactly what Norwood Sawmills is known for to this very day. In fact, we have more than fifty patents on innovative yet practical personal sawmills and components.

That's more than ALL other sawmill companies in the entire world combined!

What this means to our portable sawmill owners is that they have choices, flexibility, and endurance they can depend on with Norwood Sawmills.

It means you can start small, and work up to your changing needs because we build flexibility and growth potential into our portable sawmills with smart "add them when you need them" components.

It means you can depend on your portable sawmill lasting for a very long time and retaining its value.

And what it means to our competitors is that THEY have to figure out the second best way to accomplish anything, because they simply can't keep up with the innovations we've perfected in our portable sawmills!

We have sawmills in service in more than 100 countries, that have been working steadily since early 1993 without any issues, which is pretty remarkable all by itself.

But even more remarkable (especially these days!) is that all Norwood Sawmills are not only built to last…they are built entirely in the USA and Canada – not China, Taiwan, or Poland like the other portable sawmills out there.

That's because Norwood's philosophy is the same today as it was when Peter Dale was sweating it out in his shop over two decades ago.

We're committed to providing hard-working people like you with efficient, reliable, accurate, no-nonsense sawmilling equipment at fair prices.

We don't build super-sized, super-expensive monster mills that are anything but portable. We don't outsource to the far side of the world to try and cut corners.

And we don't mess around when it comes to quality and flat out knowing WOOD.

From that first portable sawmill that built one man's dream…to creating profitable businesses for proud sawmill owners in third world countries…to turning your backyard into a source of enduring family memories…

We Live and Breathe Portable Sawmills

We want YOU to catch the vision of what is possible with a portable sawmill too!

So what better way than to make sure you know exactly how to choose a portable sawmill, how to build a business with your sawmill if you want, or how to simply produce the smoothest, straightest, most beautiful lumber you've ever seen so you can build YOUR dream.

And that is why we have created *The Ultimate Guide to Portable Sawmills.*

Please enjoy the valuable content you will find within these pages.

It is our mission to share the fun and excitement that comes as part and parcel with portable sawmill ownership.

Yes, that's right. Portable sawmills are fun! And we sincerely hope you will find this book useful.

To your milling success,
The Norwood Team

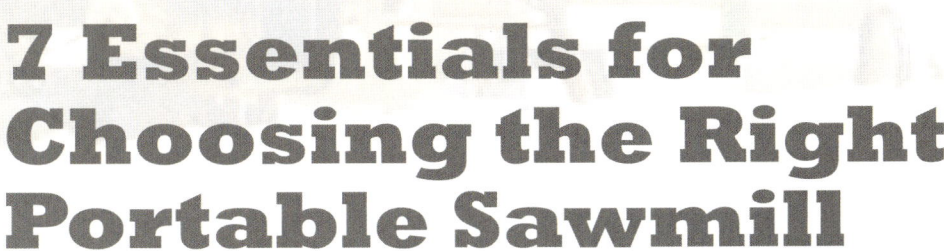

7 Essentials for Choosing the Right Portable Sawmill

When it comes to investing in a portable sawmill, it's easy to get a little confused about what you should be looking for.

And let's face it. Your investment should give you years of efficiency, productivity, and enjoyment.

You want your sawmill to perform exactly the way you need it to.

But here's the thing…what you want to do today with your sawmill can change over time as you gain experience and realize the potential at your fingertips.

For example, if you want to turn a passion for milling into a profitable business, you need to be able to scale up and handle increasing volume.

If you try your hand at building a garden bench or a shed and discover you are ready to build a vacation cabin, you want to be able to make that exciting leap without concern about log size, efficiency, or location.

Frankly, it is very common to develop such a deep connection to the rewarding fun of creating smooth as silk lumber with your sawmill that you just want to do MORE.

It's the addictive thrill of seeing your sawmill blade cut through a freshly-hewn log as smoothly as a hot knife through butter. That rush is what we sawyers refer to as having "sawdust in your veins" – and it can happen faster than you might think!

> *"I DO still like the smell of fresh sawn sawdust though. It gets in your blood and you can't seem to shake it; believe me I've tried."* — Gus, Norwood Connect

And you surely want to avoid a painful discovery AFTER you've already purchased your sawmill that you now need more capacity, power, or versatility than you ended up with.

The unfortunate condition known as "buyer's remorse" can easily be avoided if you simply do your homework before you buy.

So let's take a look at seven essential points you should definitely keep in mind when choosing your portable sawmill.

ESSENTIAL #1: Size Matters!

When purchasing a portable sawmill, the first thing you need to ask yourself is this:

"What will you be using your sawmill for?"

Are you absolutely sure you will only want it to sit in one place, or is there the possibility you might want to move it from time to time?

If you want the option to take your sawmill to various locations, this is an important consideration so you don't order a mill that will basically be rooted to the ground for the duration.

- **Will you be milling for small projects, or is there the possibility you will want to increase the scope of your creativity eventually?**

- **Does the idea of milling for others for profit get your heart racing with excitement?**

- **Or would you rather work on your own sawing lumber because it just makes you happy to see the sawdust fly?**

- **There's no right or wrong answer – it's all about what is right for YOU.**

Another aspect to keep in mind regarding how you will be using your sawmill are your natural resources.

If you have a resource of big trees and you know you're going to be cutting lumber of pretty decent size, then you're better off starting with the bigger mills right out of the gate.

Or if you're working with smaller logs and you know that's going to be your base, then you might consider the smaller unit.

If you're a woodworker, the smaller mills might suit you well to begin with.

Because yes, it really is true...

 La Segheria Mobile del Ticino - Boratt Petrolo posted a photo to Norwood Portable Sawmills's timeline – with Jean-Claude Bibo Antonioli in Ticino, Swizterland

April 10

We loves push to the limit our sawmill

Like Comment Share 👍4 💬1 ↱19

Size Matters When Choosing Your Sawmill!

You want to have a sawmill with good size capacity on the diameter it can handle.

You deserve to see the facts when it comes to capacity of your sawmill, because far too many sawmill companies have no problem exaggerating what you can do with your mill.

Be alert to this, because some major manufacturers will say you can handle the really big logs (30 or more inches in diameter), which technically may be true, but you'll spend all day doing it.

Ouch! Who wants to sweat blood all day over ONE gigantic log?

On the other hand, a sawmill with a smartly designed clamping system allows you to easily vary your capacity.

So if you have some 12-foot long logs, that are 30" in diameter, you'll be able to clamp down and mill them, just like this…

But maybe you want to switch to a different type of log after that.

Let's say your next log is only 4-feet long, but is a nice piece of walnut or cherry with a fancy grain on the inside – and your fingers are itching to release that grain as smoothly and efficiently as possible.

If you've got the right sawmill, it's not a problem. You should be able to simply move your clamps in a couple of minutes and reconfigure your sawmill to handle the different shape and size of your logs.

The main thing here is you want this transition to be super EASY and quick, so you can do what you want to do, when you want, without it being a pain.

Here are some illustrations showing what to look for in a versatile and reliable clamping system:

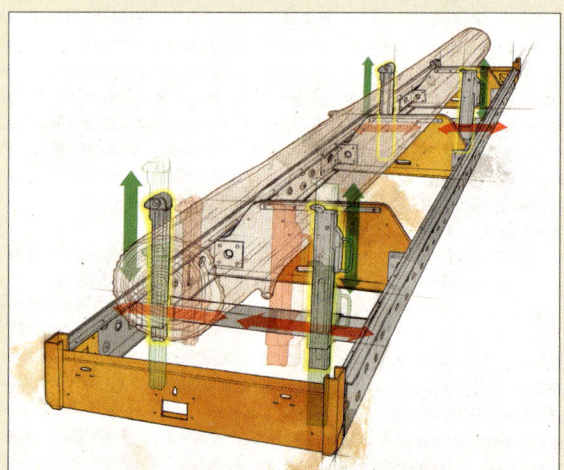

Log rests and log dogs can both move laterally and vertically.

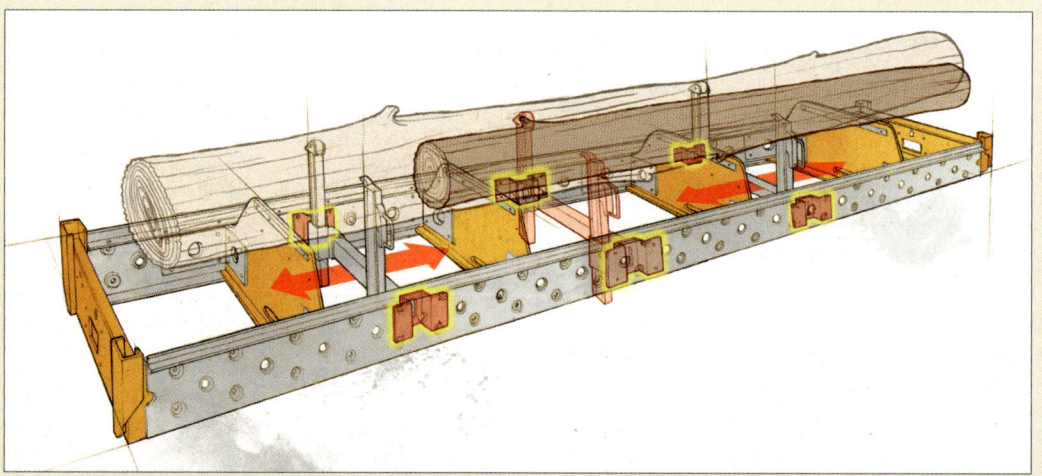

Quickly move logs clamping stations along the log deck to additional receiving stations to accommodate short or long logs.

Owning a sawmill that can handle logs from 8" in diameter on up to 36" is not only possible, it can be easy to accomplish without taking hours and hours.

Look for a portable sawmill that allows you to "grow as you go" with optional attachments like a trailer package, sawmill bed extensions, and extra log clamping stations.

If your sawmill will "sleep outside" instead of under a roof, you may want to include a cover for it that is easy to put on and off. This will save you on cables, lubricant jugs, and the overall condition of your mill.

If you are going to be working with large logs, roller toe boards may be worthwhile for you. They will allow you to perform operations that would otherwise require a helper.

Roller Toe Boards allow you to perform operations that would otherwise require a helper.

When you look at the "big picture" this way, you'll be able to choose the best sawmill for your needs right from the beginning, to accommodate the maximum size you'll be able to work with.

The other thing you want to consider is the power and speed of your sawmill.

Experienced sawyers agree...*in most cases you ought to go with the largest engine option for power.*

You'd be hard pressed to find an experienced sawyer who wishes they had LESS power than they have. But they are always glad to have as much as they can.

Even with the most powerful engines, you probably won't burn more than 2-½ gallons of fuel in a day, so they are very economical to run as well.

So keep log size, power options, and ease of milling in mind as you zero in on the right portable sawmill for your needs, and the potential to efficiently expand when and if you want.

When you do, you're very likely to choose wisely when purchasing your personal sawmill.

ESSENTIAL #2:
Flexibility Is Your Key To Happiness

As we've already touched on, being able to do what you want, when you want, is absolutely essential to being happy with your portable sawmill.

And that means you want FLEXIBILITY in the design of your sawmill.

You've had a look at one aspect of flexibility in **Essential #1** – which is the clamping system to reliably accommodate a wide variety of log sizes.

Remember, you want to own a sawmill that allows you to add on and upgrade as you wish.

You don't want to find out that "what you see is what you get" and there are no other options available for your sawmill.

And then there's the matter of **portability.**

Ideally, you don't want to have to figure out how to rig up a separate trailer if you decide you'd like to move your sawmill.

Not only is that cumbersome, it has the potential to be hazardous if your sawmill wasn't designed with the potential for portability right from the start.

When you choose a sawmill with versatile trailer options, you can easily move your sawmill by simply bolting the axles right onto the mill itself, so the sawmill actually becomes its own trailer.

Keeping it simple is so much easier for you. A trailer package like this just makes sense…

Pretty cool! And it allows you to easily transport your sawmill onto location if and when you choose to. So if you want to saw wood for others, you can go to them with your sawmill.

Remember, when you have this kind of flexibility, you don't even have to order the trailer package at first. You can start out stationary and add options like this later.

It's definitely worth considering because if you start out with a sawmill that is only meant to be stationary, you'll have to sell your mill and buy another one to become portable.

In addition, there are other add-ons you may want eventually as well.

Let's take the Norwood HD36 as our example.

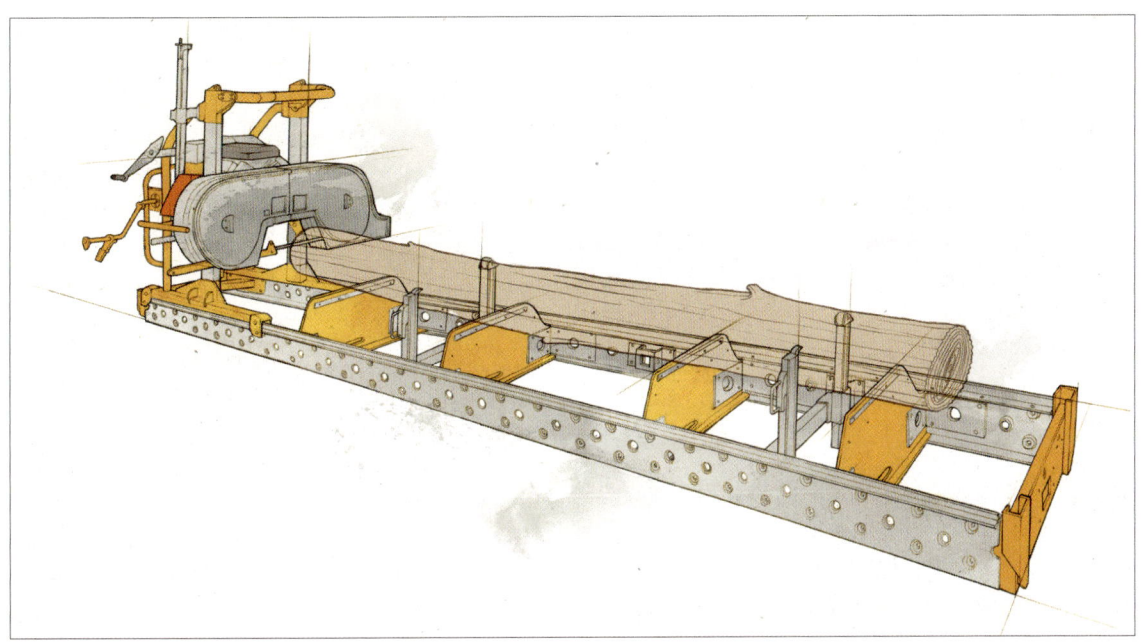

With this bad boy, you can start off as a manual mill where you load the logs by hand, turn them by hand, and push the blade through the wood by hand.

But you can add to it as you go.

You can say...

"OK, I need a log loader now."

And you can add a log loader to it like this...

Then sometime down the road, even years later, you can say…

"OK, I'm ready to add power feed to it. I can afford it, and I'm cutting some bigger volumes where it would really be effective for me."

And then you can add your power feed, just like this…

You can add roller systems, even hydraulics (sure to impress your friends and family, and ever so powerful!)

With this kind of versatility, you can end up with your dream machine. And even if you don't do it all at once…you'll know you CAN do it when you are ready.

Having that add on versatility is an important element for you.

The bottom line is this. **Don't settle for less.**

Look for the versatility and flexibility that will allow you to get everything you want on your portable sawmill, even if you are adding it piece by piece over time.

You'll come out ahead in the long run.

ESSENTIAL #3: Built To Last

It is entirely reasonable to expect years of reliable service from your portable sawmill.

Among our Norwood family (we consider our clients like family!), it is extremely common for our portable sawmills to run hard for years and years.

That's because an important element to our outlook on how sawmills are built includes planned durability, rather than planned obsolescence.

You've probably heard the expression,

"The whole is GREATER than the sum of its parts."

This is particularly true with portable sawmills.

When they are constructed with integrity and craftsmanship every step of the way, you get something much greater than mere metal, blades, nuts, and bolts.

So don't get fooled by smoke-and-mirrors marketing that hides the true quality of everything from the nuts and bolts to bigger issues like log decks and rail strength.

There are a lot of mills out there that are entirely too flimsy in their construction.

If you push them sideways, the whole thing sways on you. That's just one indication that you're not going to be able to cut straight because, with a band saw, everything has to be held rigidly in place to get a good cut.

So the design of the mill, and the construction of the unit, is paramount.

Here's a simple test if you're looking at a portable sawmill…

Push against it.
Does it give, or does it stand solid as a rock?

The rigidity of the frame when you push on it will tell you quite a bit about whether it will stand up to the type of use you're going to give it.

Lumber JACK SAYS

"*You may not know how or when, but there will be a day when you will want to do even more with your mill. There is no down-side to keeping your options open … Choosing a sawmill that offers full flexibility doesn't cost anything.*"

Think of the framework as similar to the foundation of your house. That's why you want…

Top Quality all the Way

Here are some elements of quality to look for in any portable sawmill you are considering…

✓ **LOG DECK STRENGTH:**
   Can it withstand the weight of the logs you'll put on it?

We're proud to announce Norwood's LumberPro log deck has been tested by PhD level Materials Engineers and it's official…

The Pro's log deck is **stronger than our competition and more than twice as stiff.**

That's because it is built of twin, double-plated, debossed-steel almost a full quarter of an inch thick.

Yes, these are a lot of "PhD" words! And as they say, a picture is worth a thousand words, so take a look at what we're talking about…

✓ **DURABILITY:**
   Will it last?

When you invest in a portable sawmill, you want it to work hard for you for years to come. In fact, you should be able to depend on your sawmill for the long haul. The only reason you should have to replace it is because you WANT to!

Here are some examples of the LumberMate 2000 still hard at work after fifteen years…

Above, John Depew; right, Matt Dubois; below, Ray LaPrairie.

✓ WHERE IS IT MADE?
Let's hear it for North America!

We strongly recommend you look for a quality sawmill that is manufactured from stem to stern in the USA and Canada, not in China, Taiwan, or Poland.

Be a diligent detective when it comes to where your sawmill is manufactured.

Because, unfortunately, there are other companies who claim to be "home grown" who may package their mills in North America, but are using inferior parts imported from China, Taiwan, and Poland.

It's almost a certainty that you've experienced inferior parts or components on other things you may have purchased that were constructed from substandard materials.

Not only is it disappointing and frustrating, it's basically like throwing your money onto a bonfire and watching it go up in smoke.

It doesn't take a psychological analysis to understand WHY you want your investment to be durable, reliable and functional! You want to be smart with your money, and you want the things you buy to do their job.

Sawmills take a beating. In a way, it's almost like they take on a personality as they put their "shoulder to the wheel" for you, and work hard day in and day out.

They have to handle heavy logs without complaint. They have to cut accurately in sometimes very trying conditions. They have to operate smoothly, safely, and consistently every single time.

That's why you simply cannot trust your milling to some cheap, offshore import made in a sweatshop-type factory by unskilled, low paid workers who don't really care one way or the other if your sawmill is reliable.

Yes, we're passionate about this. Because we ship our sawmills all over the globe, and have seen lives changed in Third World countries, simply by having access to a sturdy and reliable sawmill.

Belgium

Rebuilding with the United Nations in the Philippines.

Mozambique

It's not an exaggeration to say we've seen families brought closer, dreams realized, legacies fulfilled, and opportunities created... all through the ability to unleash the power of a quality portable sawmill.

And you can't trust something this important to inferior quality or careless manufacturing.

✓ **THE LONG-TERM PICTURE:**
Does it hold its value?

Unlike a car that immediately loses value the minute you drive it off the lot, a quality sawmill should hold its value even years later.

First of all, if you try to find a used Norwood, they are scarcer than hen's teeth.

But if you DO find one, it will sell for very close to what the owner paid for it. Even a LumberMate 2000 that is 15 years old goes for practically new price. In other words we're talking ZERO depreciation. It's phenomenal!

So if you invest in a portable sawmill and eventually want to sell it so you can move up into the next level, you will very likely sell your mill fast and for top dollar.

✓ **WHAT DO THEIR CUSTOMERS HAVE TO SAY?**
Don't be afraid to ask!

You should be able to access unsolicited customer comments, even talk directly to owners of the sawmill you are considering. So don't be afraid to ask!

ESSENTIAL #4: Keeping It Easy

Unless you're a glutton for punishment, you want to choose a sawmill that is very user friendly and easy to use.

• **It should be simple to run, ideally with the potential for single hand use in terms of throttle and clutch**

• **Adjustments should be very easy to do**

• **Maintenance, lubrication, and changing out blades should be very straightforward**

Your sawmill should require very little maintenance time overall.

You can accomplish this by looking for features like this:

- **Industrial Grade Powder Coat** to protect your sawmill's finish…

- **Smooth Sawhead Feed** so you can guide the sawhead through the cut with finger-tip pressure…

- **Comfort-Height Operator's Station** for your comfort…

- **Auto-Blade Lube System** to automatically deliver water directly to the blade…

- **Automated Quick-Cycle Sawing Functions** for increased productivity…

When you are considering your choice of sawmill, you should definitely ask lots of questions, especially about features like those listed here.

Don't be afraid to put your potential sawmill representative through their paces! You deserve the very best quality in your portable sawmill so you can enjoy many productive hours of milling.

ESSENTIAL #5: Keeping It Real

Certainly you want to be seen and recognized as a real person when it comes to support with your sawmill. This is another reason why having a very well established company with a strong track record and one with strong roots in your own country is preferred.

Here are some elements to look for that will assure you are well taken care of…

- **Knowledgeable customer service readily available to you from native English speakers who are sawmill experts, not robotic "phone jockeys".**

- **Direct shipping of your sawmill to your location anyplace in the world.**

- **The option to have your sawmill pre-assembled if you wish.**

- **Easy, clear, assembly instructions written in native English.**

- **Free access to an online community of like-minded people who love to talk sawmilling!**

- **The assurance of a written warranty covering your sawmill.**

- **The protection of a money-back guarantee assuring your 100% satisfaction.**

It's easy to let this aspect of choosing your portable sawmill to get lost in the shuffle, but it is ever so important. Look for a strong track record of support in ALL of these areas and you'll have a much more rewarding experience with your milling.

ESSENTIAL #6: Keeping It Safe

It goes without saying that you want to be able to operate your portable sawmill safely.

This goes beyond wearing eye protection and close toed shoes when operating your sawmill. And it's another reason you should want the assurance of a team dedicated to the highest quality in designing and building your portable sawmill.

You should only consider a sawmill built to International Safety Standards.

This means integrated safety features such as…

- **Full sawmill blade protection**

- **Safety-switch equipped guards**

- **Rapid blade-brake**

Here's a quick little story that will illustrate the importance of this.

One of our Norwood sawmill owners had a very eye-opening experience. He is an expert sawyer, and was talking to some business owners from Finland.

They said were looking at other portable sawmills in comparison to Norwood sawmills, and quite frankly they were shocked.

They stated, "*You couldn't even sell these other sawmills in our country. It would not be allowed because they are too dangerous.*"

And that should concern you.

At Norwood, we are extremely proud of our track record of safety.

Norwood sawmills are specifically designed for use around the globe. You can go to any country in the world, and a Norwood sawmill will meet or exceed their safety requirements. You should expect no less in a portable sawmill for your personal use.

ESSENTIAL #7: Proven Innovative Technology

Last but not least, you should be looking for the highest level of proven innovative technology in your sawmill.

Perhaps you're thinking, "*But it's only a sawmill, and I'm not a techie!*"

First of all, innovative technology doesn't mean YOU have to know how to design it. All you have to do is take advantage of it and **let it work for you!**

Sawing isn't complicated. It involves a lot of repetition – load logs, square log, slice boards, stack lumber. Almost anyone can do it and everyone has a lot of fun doing it.

LumberPro HD36
NORWOOD

⚠ **NORWOOD** ®
SAWMILLS

NorwoodSawmills.com / 800•567•0404

U.S. Patent Nos. 7,784,387, 11/005,186, 8,215, 216, 8,261,645, 8,261,647, 12/949,877, D639,319 & D654,101, Canada Patent Nos. 2,488,216, 132823, 2,687,619, 2,687,622, 2,687,623, 2,688,407, 2,696,974, 2,782,909 & 134185; EU Patent Nos. 001212393-0001 & 001217277-0001; Brazil Patent No. DI 7001877-4; Other patents pending in multiple jurisdictions.

Part No: LM34-PS-001

With each cut comes more repetition – unlock sawhead, adjust depth of cut, relock sawhead, turn on blade lube, cut, turn off blade lube and return.

But what if your sawmill looked after one of those tasks for you? You would save valuable time on every single cut. What if your sawmill looked after two of those tasks? How about three? Or four? **That adds up to serious time saved – and a serious boost in the size of your stack of boards, at the end of the day.**

That's the kind of innovation Norwood builds into their band sawmills. Nothing fancy – just good old-fashioned "out-of-the-box" thinking that makes Norwood bandmills hands-down more productive than the rest.

Second, if you want your investment in a portable sawmill to pay you back in dividends for years and years, *you NEED that technology built right into the tough as nails components of your sawmill.*

And this is yet another reason you should never settle for substandard components, cheap parts, or inferior construction that may be hidden just beneath the surface of your sawmill.

Look for a sawmill manufacturer who is actively investing in top-quality parts and fabrication technologies such as...

- **3-dimension (5-axis) laser and standard laser**

- **Computer numerical control machining**

- **Industrial-grade, rust-resistant powder-coating**

- **Precision-extrusion**

- **Robotic welding**

- **Zinc-dichromate plating**

- **Precision-balanced cast-iron**

- **High-grade, heavy-gauge steel**

In addition, you should expect your sawmill to be the product of consistent research and innovation in design.

This isn't about unnecessary bells and whistles.

This is about...

- Constantly pursuing **a high level of thoughtful design** that takes into consideration exactly how you actually use your portable sawmill...

- **Serving you** in the best possible way...

- **Maximizing the value** of your wood...

- Making it **reliably easy for you to be successful** with your milling...

And now you are better prepared to go forth and choose your portable sawmill with the assurance that you know what to look for.

If you let these 7 Essentials guide you, you'll soon be on your way to many satisfying years of milling!

Lumber JACK SAYS

"Your sawmill has to get jobs done... and get them done efficiently, reliably and safely. Make sure the important "MUST HAVES" get checked off your sawmill wish-list:

❑ *Is it safe?*

❑ *Is it (and is the company that made it) reliable?*

❑ *Is it easy (and fun) to use?*

❑ *Is it efficient (does it automatically look after a lot of those time-wasting operations)?*

❑ *Is it versatile (can you upgrade and add attachments)?"*

Milling for Money:

Turn Your Portable Sawmill Into A Profitable Business

There's a profitable phenomenon growing steadily that just could be the answer you've been looking for…

The Increasing Demand For Custom Milling

In fact, in recent years, portable sawmills have become a profitable ticket to entrepreneurship for motivated portable sawmill owners.

In the old days, sawing was a slow and difficult process requiring several brawny men to produce any boards at all by literally pulling and pushing the saw. Eventually, the arrival of the first basic sawmills was a giant step forward in the development of frontier communities.

Fortunately, we've come a very long way from those early days!

And now, thanks to technology, the portability and flexibility of a well-designed portable sawmill means things are much easier. And there's a growing trend you can capitalize on either as a part-time sideline, or even a new fulltime moneymaker.

You see, the delivery of a valuable service that used to be labor intensive and complicated has become safe, streamlined, and accessible to regular folks who would love to create a thriving custom sawing business, like Russell Frye of New York is planning to do…

"I am very pleased with my LumberMate 2000. I have saved a great deal of lumber with it, with no major problems or breakdowns. It's a great mill and I've turned a hobby into a custom-sawing business. I'm going to retire in three years from my regular job and then work my sawmill business full time. Thank you for a good sawmill and a good investment."

If you're looking for a solid justification for portable sawmill ownership, this should make you very happy – because today's portable sawmills like the Norwood LumberMan MN26 all the way up to our LumberPro HD36 each hold the possibility of successful entrepreneurship within their powerful components.

Mills like these are **perfect** for producing volumes of boards, or for specialty milling such as oversized lumber.

There are many reasons why the interest in turning your portable sawmill into a profitable business is at an all-time high. Maybe one of these scenarios fits the bill for you…

- Like Russell, **you're retired or getting ready to retire**, and are still in good health and would like to earn additional income…

- You've been downsized, or downright ousted from your job and you are **looking for a new way to make money…**

- You've fallen in love with milling wood (or are about to!) and think it would be extremely cool to **make money doing something you are passionate about…**

- You're sick of being a desk jockey and **you want to have a more active, outdoor lifestyle…**

- **You enjoy working with your hands…**

- **You just happen to own acres of trees…**

- **You live where OTHER people have acres of trees…**

- **You want to build a house or have access to other people who want to build a house…**

- **You secretly think plaid flannel shirts are awesome.** ☺

There are definitely even more reasons than this. The bottom line is portable sawmills are now filling the niche that the traditional forest industry has lost – and savvy folks with the desire to be their own boss are leveraging that to their advantage.

So let's take a look at whether turning portable sawmill ownership into a business is right for you, starting with…

3 Simple Steps to Success

STEP 1: Choose your portable sawmill

Choose wisely! Lack of foresight about how you'll be using your portable sawmill can cost you dearly down the road.

On the other hand, choosing the right portable sawmill for the job can pay you back in big dividends! If you haven't read through it already, be sure you check back on **Chapter One, *"7-Tips For Choosing The Right Portable Sawmill"*** for helpful tips and things to consider.

For example, a huge benefit to your portable sawmill business is being just that… PORTABLE!

So you'll want a sawmill that not only has the flexibility to add components later as you need them, but is also built to be completely and EASILY portable too, just like this…

As we'll discuss in just a minute, that portability is also a built-in advertisement for your business, and can attract new customers surprisingly quickly and easily too.

STEP 2: Get addicted to sawmilling!

Seriously, this is one "incurable disease" you'll want. You may recall in the Introduction to this book we said portable sawmills are FUN, and we weren't kidding!

Once you get sawdust flowing in your veins, you'll be hooked for life. But no worries…this condition is easily treated with regular doses of woodcutting.

And there's simply no better feeling than making money in the process!

If your dream is to LOVE what you do and make a healthy income in the process, this could be the answer you've been looking for.

STEP 3: Plan for success by making a plan.

Obviously you need to have some idea of how you'll create your business. This chapter is devoted to helping you on that path.

Let's just stop for a moment here to speak to a question you may already have floating around in your brain.

YES you can do this even if you've never been a lumberjack, or you grew up on the mean streets of the city instead of chopping down trees with your trusty axe!

With the incredible leaps forward we've made with technology and design, you can BECOME a milling expert in short order when you take advantage of everything the right kind of portable sawmill can do for you.

So let's get to it!

> *"A fantastic thing happened: I opened my mailbox and found a note from someone asking if I could cut hemlock for a horse barn. People starting stopping by asking me to cut wood for their fences, bandstands and other projects. Most recently I was asked to make side boards for dump trucks. I have not done any advertising and yet people came … and they still come.*
>
> *The people I have met are from all walks of life: judges, loggers, artists, business owners. They are always nice and so grateful for the wood. I mill for fun but, if I wanted to run a business, I could do it without trying. I have gone to farmers markets and, when artisans there find out I have a sawmill, they ask me if I will cut for them. It happens so much I am taken aback by the amount of opportunity … All because of an orange sawmill."*
>
> — Kevin Kesick, NY

The very first question that usually pops up when considering using your portable sawmill to build a business is this...

"How much can I make?"

While we can't really predict how much you will make, we can certainly show you a few examples of what is possible with a little ingenuity and creative thinking.

For example, after Hurricane Sandy, a sawmill owner by the name of Dan Richfield saw an opportunity in the tens of thousands of downed and damaged trees.

Dan and his partner worked out a way to obtain a great deal of the wood, mostly for free. They stacked a two-year supply of wood on their lot, and now mill the wood into slabs they sell for tabletops after drying the wood.

He states a simple table top from common salvaged wood like Red Oak goes for as much as $1,000 and they sell as many as 50 a month. You do the math!

Scott Schaeffer is running his successful mobile sawmilling business, Wilfer Mobile Sawmills, in Colorado.

Then there's Frank and Dan Myers from California who are happily using their Norwood Portable Sawmill to make money.

Remember what we said about starting from scratch? Dan states he had NO experience cutting prior to starting this business with his uncle Frank less than two years ago, but now is sawing like a pro, creating everything from furniture to lumber for building houses.

When asked about his choice for a Norwood portable sawmill Frank Myers stated,

> *"This mill has been a great asset to my family. It's just like money in the bank. If you've got an imagination, it opens a whole new world for anything you want to build or create."*

In fact, when it comes to owning a portable sawmill Frank doesn't mince words. He says…

"Buy One Today. Make Money Tomorrow."

Sounds like a plan! So here are some things to keep in mind.

Getting Started & Growing Your Business

After you become the proud owner of your new portable band sawmill, you'll probably find it doesn't take long before people begin coming out of the woodwork, asking you to saw up a tree or two for them.

It might be a tree that died or blew down, or it might be that they have a specific project in mind. Many sawmill owners can verify that before they knew it, they were already in business!

This is a perfect way to…

Start Your Sawmill Business Part-Time

Running your mill in your spare time for fun and profit is a great way to test the waters before making the leap into a full-scale sawmill business.

It gives you a chance to hone your sawmilling skills, learn tricks that will boost production, and identify possible pitfalls you want to avoid.

Even if you aren't looking to quit your day job, sawmilling can be an incredibly satisfying and reliable way to supplement your family income.

But you just might find you are having so much fun milling part-time, you're ready to…

GROW Your Sawmilling Business

To be a successful entrepreneur, you need to understand how these three elements fit together to build a sturdy foundation for your new business.

✓ 1. RAW MATERIALS:

If your business model involves selling boards, you need a reliable source of quality raw materials (logs). Make sure the cost of goods (the price you pay) allows you to price your end product competitively.

✓ 2. EFFICIENT PRODUCTION:

To maximize profits, you need to maximize production.

To maximize production, you need to maximize efficiency.

To do this, you need:

A) An efficient sawmill

B) An efficient operation

The importance of choosing the right portable sawmill cannot be overstated!

- It must have **fast cycle times.**

- It must **minimize operator workload.**

- It must be **flexible enough to grow** as your sawmilling operation expands.

This might be a good time to go back over ***Chapter 1*** as you consider the possibilities for growing your business.

✓ 3. MARKETING:

Now don't get nervous about this one! It's important to your business, but it doesn't have to be overwhelming either.

You can start as simply as putting your ad on Craigslist. This can be very effective.

You can run ads in your local paper, and put ads on the bulletin boards of farm stores in your area,

But the most effective way to build your business is the power of word of mouth. Once you have a few happy customers, you will be amazed how word travels as they refer others to you. It is the most powerful element for building your business.

And don't overlook the power of being PORTABLE!

You'll read more about this in a moment, but for now, let's just say when you are pulling a portable sawmill down the road, you automatically attract NEW customers.

At this point you may be wondering what type of business model would be the best fit for you. So let's take a look at...

Three Smart Sawmill Business Models

The three most common ways to make money sawmilling are:

1. Stationary Custom Milling

2. Portable Custom Milling

3. Become the Lumber Yard

Many successful full-time sawyers use one or a combination of these business models. And before we go any further, let's examine our personal favorite for getting to where you are making money as quickly as possible.

Get PORTABLE!

When you go into business, it should go without saying that you want to offer the highest value to your customers and leave them happy campers who refer others to you as well.

And the number one thing that is the easiest way to stand out for delivery of high value is to offer a portable sawmill service.

When you do this, you go to your customer's site and do the work there.

You see, a lot of people just need a few logs milled. For example, homeowners don't usually have the means of hauling logs to a sawmill and don't want to either.

All they want is the mill to arrive to where the log is. Plus, a lot of them like to help out a bit around the mill, so they can say they helped saw the log. To offer that service is probably the single biggest thing you could do.

Of course that means you need a vehicle capable of towing the sawmill. The standard Norwood HD36 weighs less than 2,000 pounds and it tows easily without having a huge vehicle. A half-ton truck would move it along nicely.

This is definitely something to keep in mind when you are purchasing your portable sawmill so you don't find you have made a costly mistake by investing in a sawmill that can't be moved easily.

Besides great customer service, the very act of towing your sawmill down the road is like a giant magnet for new customers!

We hear many stories of sawmill owners who simply were stopping to fuel up their vehicle and were immediately attracting new customers when they saw the sawmill.

But these three business models are not the only ways to make money with a sawmill. You may have other very profitable opportunities available specifically to you. For example…

- You may have a **special skillset** like carpentry, woodworking skills, or log home building…

- There may be **specific special needs of customers** in your geographic area…

- You may have **access to high-value logs** in your area, like walnut, teak, or maple.

All of these factors should be taken into consideration when deciding what business model will work best for you and your circumstances.

Again, it is crucial to choose your sawmill wisely based on your circumstances and sawmilling goals. You want a portable sawmill you can upgrade when you see new business opportunities presenting themselves.

You never want to pass up a new profitable line of sawmilling work because your sawmill cannot rise to the occasion.

Now let's look at the advantages and disadvantages of each of the three smart sawmilling business models.

✓ 1. STATIONARY CUSTOM MILLING

By far, the simplest sawmill business is custom-sawing a customer's logs, especially if they bring them to you.

ADVANTAGES:

- No log procurement costs

- Immediate payment on completion of the job

- No storage of logs or lumber

WHAT TO WATCH FOR:

- You need good access to your sawmill area

- Some customers may have difficulty transporting logs to you

HOW TO CHARGE:

- By the board foot (or cubic meter)

- By the hour

- By the job

- Include charges for blade damage due to metal strikes

✓ 2. PORTABLE CUSTOM MILLING

As mentioned, with a portable sawmill you bring your machine to the customer, eliminating the need to move logs.

ADVANTAGES:

- No log procurement costs

- Immediate payment on completion of the job

- No storage of logs or lumber

- Customers do not need to transport logs

WHAT TO WATCH FOR:

- Some customers may not have adequate access for your sawmill

- Some customers may not have adequate space for your sawmill

HOW TO CHARGE:

- By the board foot (or cubic meter)

- By the hour

- By the job

- Include charges for mileage and set-up time

- Include charges for blade damage due to metal strikes

✓ 3. "BECOME" THE LUMBER YARD

Mill lumber in anticipation of demand and store it so that it is available for customers to buy it at their leisure. In essence, you are the lumberyard, and you set the prices!

ADVANTAGES:

- You can saw ahead even without specific lumber orders

- You make it easy for customers to buy spur of the moment

- Price is 2 to 4 times what you would charge for custom-cut wood right off the mill

- You can charge even more for additional processing (drying and planing)

WHAT TO WATCH FOR:

- You need to properly store lumber for extended periods of time

- Delayed payment until wood is sold

- Log procurement costs and logistics

- Forecast customer preferences in terms of species and dimensions

HOW TO CHARGE:

- By the board foot (or cubic meter)

Now that your creative juices are flowing, you're ready for the most important advice we can possibly offer you on creating a profitable business with your portable sawmill...

You don't make money from your sawmill...

You make money from your CUSTOMERS!

Never forget your sawmill is the tool you use to provide your customers with a valuable product, and you with an income.

Follow these three simple golden rules to create the kind of iron clad loyalty that keeps your customers coming back for more, AND referring their circle of friends, relatives, and neighbors to you.

We know these Golden Rules work, because it's what we live and breathe here at Norwood Sawmills. It's our foundation, our promise, and our commitment.

And it's totally scalable, it's powerful, and enduring, no matter if you are an entrepreneur working on your own, or a thriving corporation.

Golden Rule #1:

Do what you say you'll do when you say you'll do it!

This means being there on time, finishing on time even if you are working by floodlights to do it, and putting blade sharpening ahead of TV time so you're ready for your next job.

If your customers can't depend on you, they will find another sawyer or buy their lumber elsewhere.

Scott Shaeffer ▸ **Norwood Portable Sawmills**
May 19 · Aurora, CO, United States · 🌐

Milled up 4 walnut trees today. Customer had tons of fun watching the mill and seeing all that nice lumber piling up!

Golden Rule #2:

Be professional.

Sounds simple, but this is often overlooked by sloppy business practices, a grubby appearance, or substandard equipment.

Put things in writing, even for small jobs, so everyone is literally on the same page with no unexpected surprises.

Paying attention to the small details reinforces your reputation as a professional, like using pre-printed invoices where you only need to fill in the job details and amount due.

Always pay attention to the safety of your customer and bystanders. If the customer tries to help wearing open-toe sandals or beach flip-flops, stands too close to the sawdust chute, or moves into the path of a rolling log, immediately stop and remedy the situation.

Golden Rule #3:

Follow Up.

Again, this is a simple thing to do, but extremely powerful for building your business because so many business folks don't do it. Believe it or not, you will stand out from the crowd!

Note on your calendar a date to call your customers back to see if they have any questions about the wood you have milled for them.

Let your customers know if you come across a particularly awesome piece of wood they might be interested in.

You'll be surprised how many times your customers will respond by buying more wood from you, or booking another custom milling session!

The bottom line is…

You Can Do It!

Thousands of people around the world use their portable sawmills every day to make an excellent income.

And you can too!

With the right portable sawmill and motivation, there is no limit to the possibilities out there for you.

3 Build Your World

There are many good reasons to own a portable sawmill, and one of the best is so you can enjoy the fun and satisfaction of literally building your world.

As mentioned in the Introduction to this book, the founder of Norwood Sawmills dreamed of building a cabin in the woods.

That dream was so compelling and insistent; it literally became the "mother of invention" that not only resulted in a rustic family retreat, but an entire industry as well.

But Peter Dale is hardly alone in his desire to build something enduring from the ground up with his own two hands. For more than two decades, we've helped meet the need so many have for the satisfaction and fulfillment that comes from building beautiful, serviceable, and unique creations with the wood milled on your portable sawmill.

From the most basic garden benches, to decks, floors, furniture and cabins, you can do just about anything you can imagine with your portable sawmill, just like these sawmill owners have…

"Last August I purchased a mill from Norwood. Best thing since sliced bread! Built a 24' x 32' cottage with 17' high cathedral ceiling. The mill paid for itself by now."
— Rick Montreuil, ON

So let's explore a few projects you might find of interest too!

"It has been my dream for years to build a cabin up in the mountains. With your fantastic machine, this dream is now a reality. Thanks for making this possible."

— Don Tamminga,
New Mexico

PROJECT #1: Mill Shed

When you've invested in your portable sawmill, protecting it from the elements should be a high priority.

Even if you don't have your sawmill yet, this shed is still a pretty good construction project.

The open design should be oriented so the prevailing wind hits the covered sides.

The side opening needs to be wide enough for the longest log your mills can handle. A roller or conveyer to move boards and slabs off the end of the mill will cut down on your time and effort.

The low open area behind the mill will make sawdust removal much faster.

The open design also allows plenty of fresh air to reduce any potential problems with exhaust fumes.

This design has a 20' opening, 6'6" high.

It uses only a few different dimensions of lumber.

While the sides could be built with sheet metal, once you get your mill up and running, the boards will stack up quickly.

There are many variations for a Mill Shed, but the main thing is to have adequate bracing.

Sliding doors for the front and a canvas flap on the low open side will do an even better job of protecting your mill.

The wood siding provides plenty of places to hang tools and sawmill blades, and it would be easy to build a shop or office onto the shed.

Electric lights will come in handy, and some sawyers have installed an overhead winch to load and turn the logs, as well as to move the heavier beams.

For areas with heavy snow loads, consider a truss roof with a steep pitch to shed the snow.

Always check building codes in your area before starting construction.

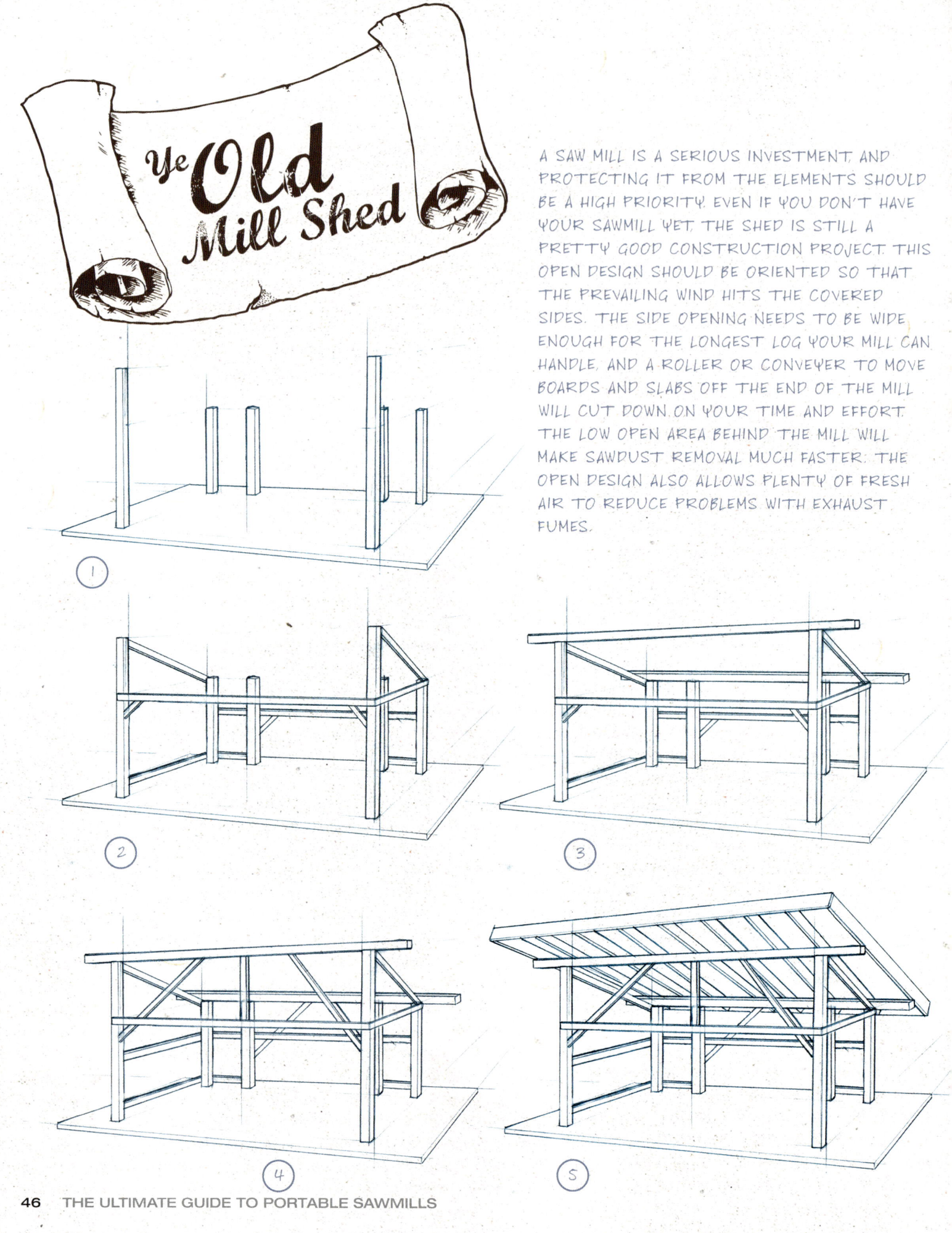

Ye Old Mill Shed

A SAW MILL IS A SERIOUS INVESTMENT, AND PROTECTING IT FROM THE ELEMENTS SHOULD BE A HIGH PRIORITY. EVEN IF YOU DON'T HAVE YOUR SAWMILL YET, THE SHED IS STILL A PRETTY GOOD CONSTRUCTION PROJECT. THIS OPEN DESIGN SHOULD BE ORIENTED SO THAT THE PREVAILING WIND HITS THE COVERED SIDES. THE SIDE OPENING NEEDS TO BE WIDE ENOUGH FOR THE LONGEST LOG YOUR MILL CAN HANDLE, AND A ROLLER OR CONVEYER TO MOVE BOARDS AND SLABS OFF THE END OF THE MILL WILL CUT DOWN ON YOUR TIME AND EFFORT. THE LOW OPEN AREA BEHIND THE MILL WILL MAKE SAWDUST REMOVAL MUCH FASTER. THE OPEN DESIGN ALSO ALLOWS PLENTY OF FRESH AIR TO REDUCE PROBLEMS WITH EXHAUST FUMES.

THIS DESIGN HAS A 20' OPENING, 6' 6" HIGH. IT USES ONLY A FEW DIFFERENT DIMENSIONS OF LUMBER. WHILE THE SIDES COULD BE BUILT WITH SHEET METAL, ONCE YOU GET THE MILL UP AND RUNNING, THE BOARDS WILL STACK UP QUICKLY.

THERE ARE MANY VARIATIONS, BUT THE MAIN THING IS TO HAVE ADEQUATE BRACING. SLIDING DOORS FOR THE FRONT AND A CANVAS FLAP ON THE LOW OPEN SIDE, FOR EXAMPLE, WILL DO AN EVEN BETTER JOB OF PROTECTING YOUR MILL. THE WOOD SIDING PROVIDES PLENTY OF PLACES TO HANG TOOLS AND SAWMILL BLADES, AND IT WOULD BE EASY TO BUILD A SHOP OR OFFICE ONTO THE SHED. ELECTRIC LIGHTS WILL COME IN HANDY, AND SOME SAWYERS HAVE INSTALLED AN OVERHEAD WINCH TO LOAD AND TURN LOGS, AND MOVE THE HEAVIER BEAMS. FOR AREAS WITH HEAVY SNOW LOADS, CONSIDER A TRUSS ROOF WITH A STEEP PITCH TO SHED THE SNOW. YOU MAY ALSO NEED TO CHECK WITH BUILDING CODES IN YOUR AREA BEFORE STARTING CONSTRUCTION.

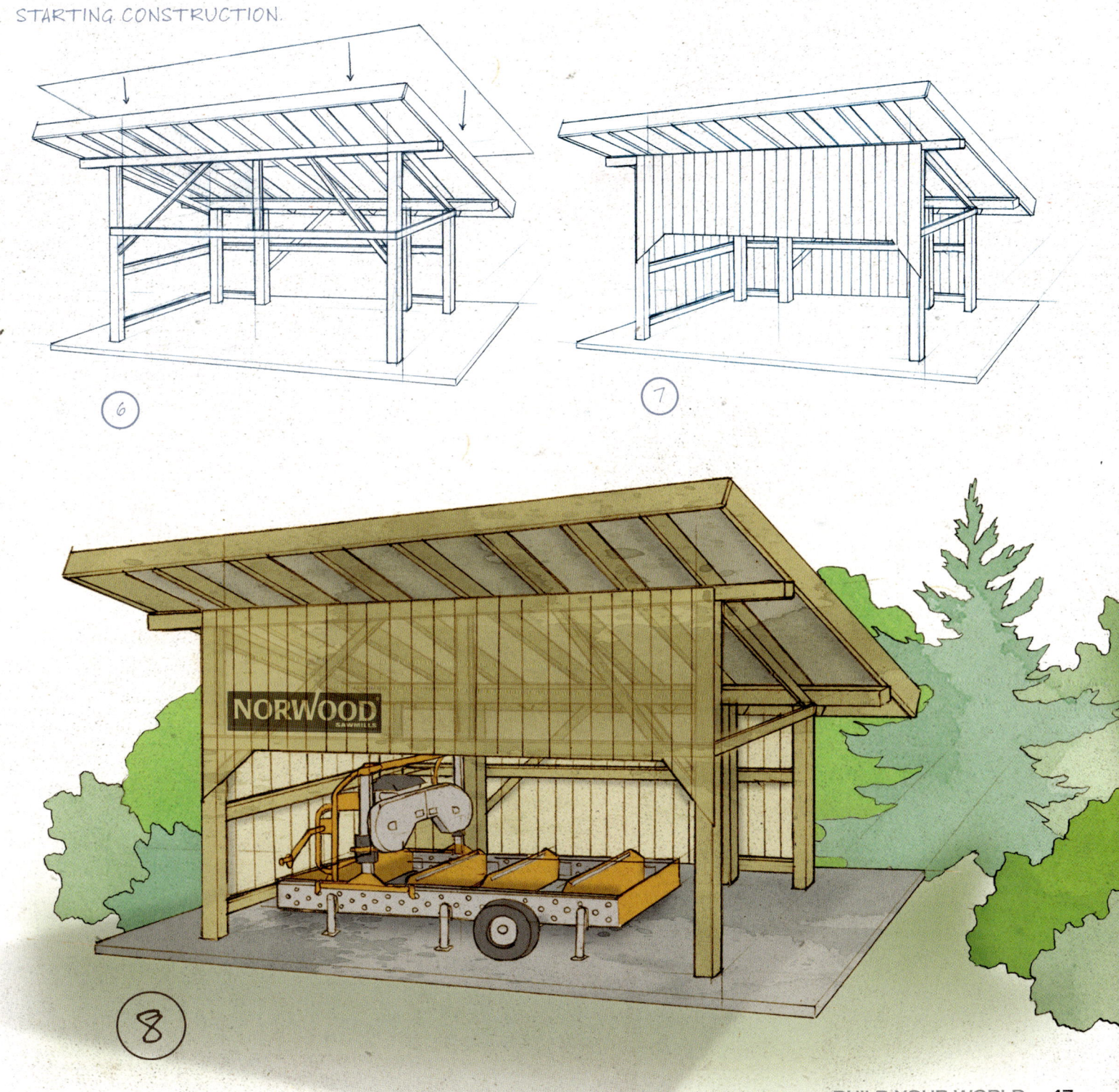

PROJECT #2: Garden or Tool Shed

Now that you've got your sawmill covered, how about moving on to your garden?

If you're interested in trying your hand at post and beam construction, this design offers a great opportunity.

You'll find your sawmill speeds up the process considerably by allowing you to make precise cuts that are difficult and time consuming with conventional tools.

Also, you have the added benefit of being able to regroup if you happen to mis-cut a beam. All you have to do is re-saw it for siding and mill another beam.

So very little goes to waste!

This shed could easily be modified to be a guest cabin, play house, chicken coop, or potting shed.

It is built on 6" x 6" beams, so it can be moved if necessary.

The top window provides light, and you can add eaves-trough and barrels to collect rain for watering the garden.

The board and batten siding is an old-time technique that lets you put up the siding fresh from the mill. As the boards shrink, a little space opens up between them. The 3" wide battens go over the cracks to seal them.

You can do this anytime, but a lot of people like to give the boards a chance to shrink before putting up the battens.

Lumber JACK SAYS

"Just use one nail for each place you attach a board to a stringer. The board will shrink sideways around the nail. If you use two nails, the board will crack as it shrinks.

Turn the boards so that the head of the nail is against the inside of the growth rings (the side of the board that was closer to the center of the tree). That way, as the board dries and tries to cup, it will pull tight against the head of the nail."

Garden Shed

IF YOU ARE INTERESTED IN TRYING YOUR HAND AT POST AND BEAM CONSTRUCTION, THIS TOOL SHED OFFERS A GREAT OPPORTUNITY. THE SAWMILL SPEEDS THE PROCESS CONSIDERABLY BY ALLOWING YOU TO MAKE PRECISE CUTS THAT ARE DIFFICULT AND TIME CONSUMING WITH CONVENTIONAL TOOLS. AND IF YOU MIS-CUT A BEAM, YOU CAN RESAW IT FOR SIDING AND MILL ANOTHER BEAM. VERY LITTLE GOES TO WASTE! THIS SHED COULD EASILY BE MODIFIED TO BE A GUEST CABIN, PLAY HOUSE, CHICKEN COOP, OR POTTING SHED. IT WAS BUILT ON 6" BY 6" BEAMS SO THAT IT CAN BE MOVED, IF NECESSARY. THE TOP WINDOW PROVIDES LIGHT AND YOU CAN ADD GUTTERS AND BARRELS TO COLLECT RAIN FOR WATERING THE GARDEN.

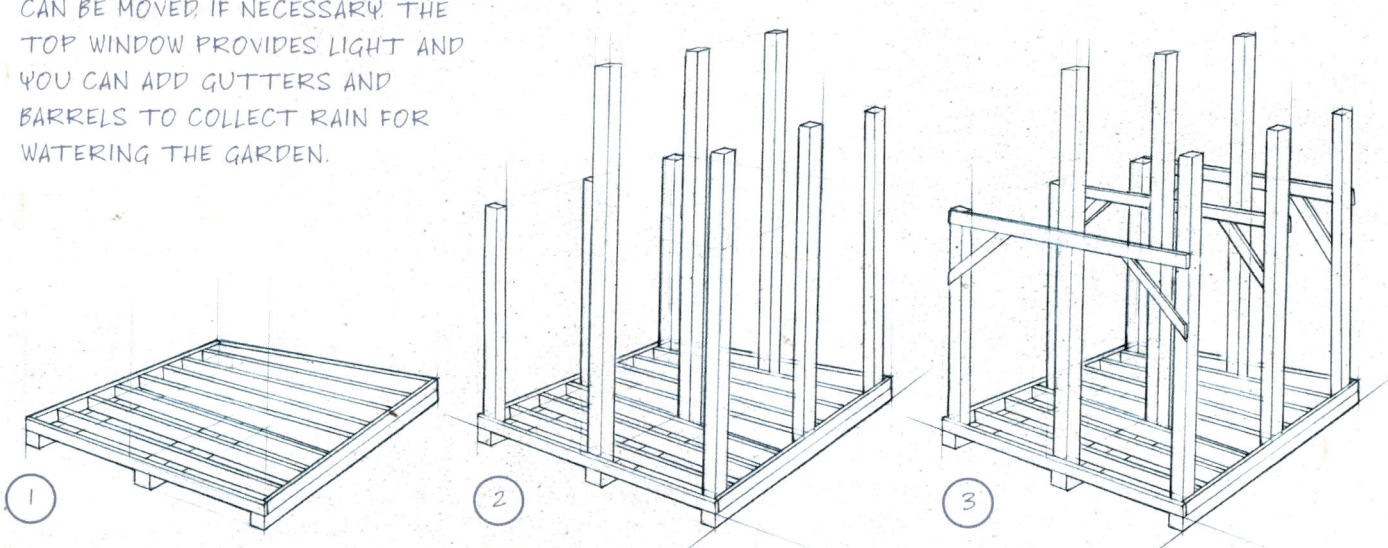

THE BOARD AND BATTON SIDING IS AN OLD TIME TECHNIQUE THAT LETS YOU PUT UP THE SIDING FRESH FROM THE MILL. AS THE BOARDS SHRINK, A LITTLE SPACE OPENS UP BETWEEN THEM. THE 3" WIDE BATTONS GO OVER THE CRACKS TO SEAL THEM. YOU CAN DO THIS ANY TIME, BUT A LOT OF PEOPLE LIKE TO GIVE THE BOARDS A CHANCE TO SHRINK BEFORE PUTTING UP THE BATTONS.

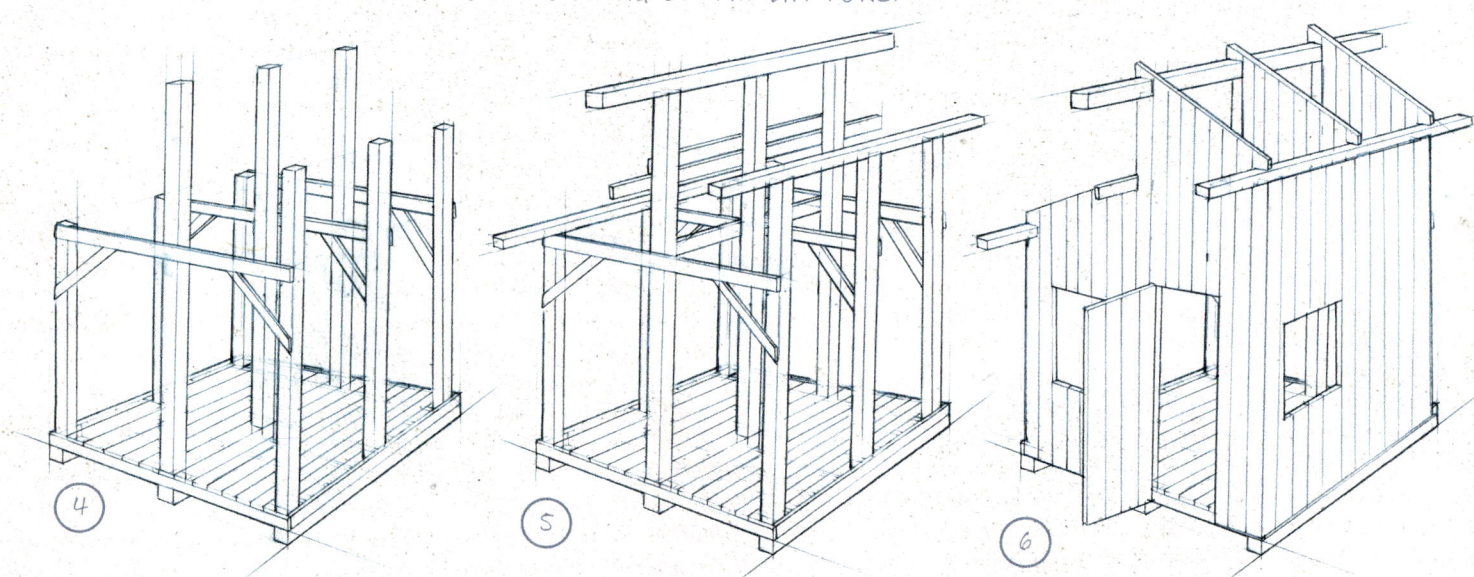

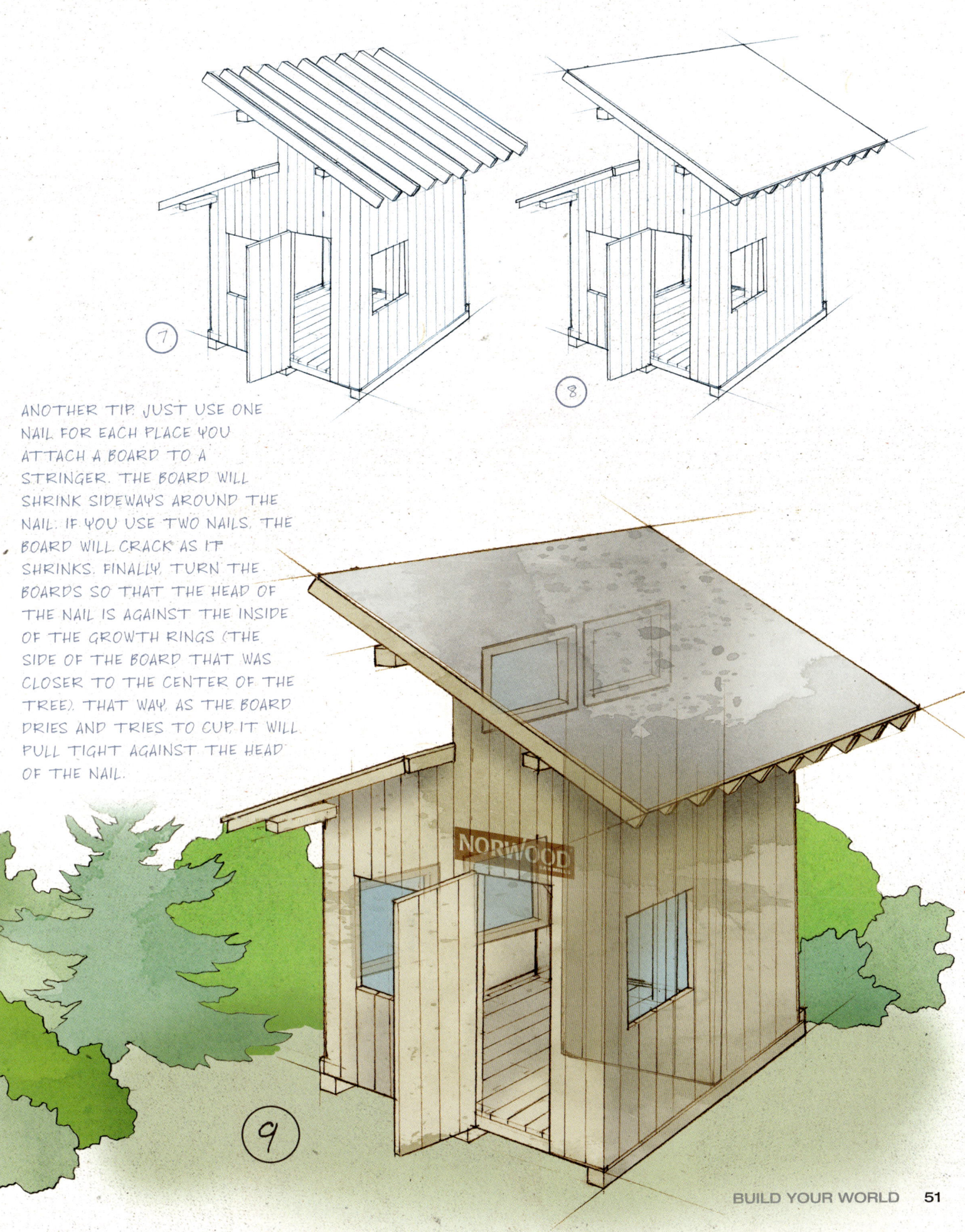

ANOTHER TIP: JUST USE ONE
NAIL FOR EACH PLACE YOU
ATTACH A BOARD TO A
STRINGER. THE BOARD WILL
SHRINK SIDEWAYS AROUND THE
NAIL. IF YOU USE TWO NAILS, THE
BOARD WILL CRACK AS IT
SHRINKS. FINALLY, TURN THE
BOARDS SO THAT THE HEAD OF
THE NAIL IS AGAINST THE INSIDE
OF THE GROWTH RINGS (THE
SIDE OF THE BOARD THAT WAS
CLOSER TO THE CENTER OF THE
TREE). THAT WAY, AS THE BOARD
DRIES AND TRIES TO CUP, IT WILL
PULL TIGHT AGAINST THE HEAD
OF THE NAIL.

PROJECT #3: Play House

There's nothing quite as special as seeing a child's face light up with joy when they discover their very own play house.

Of course this play house can also become anything from the lookout on a pirate ship to a fort. So there is tremendous versatility in this design.

This is so much better than any hypnotic electronic toy that does all the pretending for you. A playhouse like this allows the children most precious to you to explore the vast universe of their imagination.

What could be better than that?

This playhouse is designed to be 7' off the ground. This makes it easy to mow under, plus offers plenty of opportunities for slides, ropes, ladders, and other smart ways to get kids working off their extra energy.

It is 12' long overall, with an 8' observation deck (to watch the horizon for incoming ships!), and a 4' shelter just perfect for everything from afternoon tea parties to mapping out trails through the wilderness.

Posts should be at least 24" into the ground, and set in cement for stability.

The posts are the only part that need to be built of durable lumber – either treated or rot resistant species such as white oak, black locust, Osage orange, cedar or redwood.

You'll find another great thing about having your own sawmill is that you can mill whatever you need and put it up as you cut it.

In fact, you can often accomplish this in less time than it would take to go the lumber yard and sort through boards of inconsistent quality that seem to get smaller and more crooked every time!

THE ULTIMATE PLAY HOUSE

THIS PLAY HOUSE CAN BE ANYTHING FROM THE LOOKOUT ON A PIRATE SHIP TO A FORT. THIS ONE IS 7' OFF THE GROUND TO MAKE IT EASY TO MOW UNDER, AND OFFERS PLENTY OF OPPORTUNITIES FOR SLIDES, ROPES, LADDERS, AND OTHER WAYS TO GET THE YOUNG ONES TO WORK OFF THEIR EXTRA ENERGY. THIS ONE IS 12' LONG OVERALL WITH AN 8' OBSERVATION DECK AND 4' SHELTER

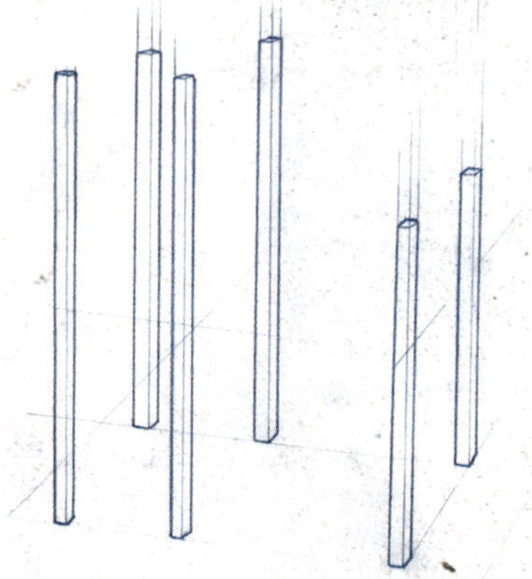

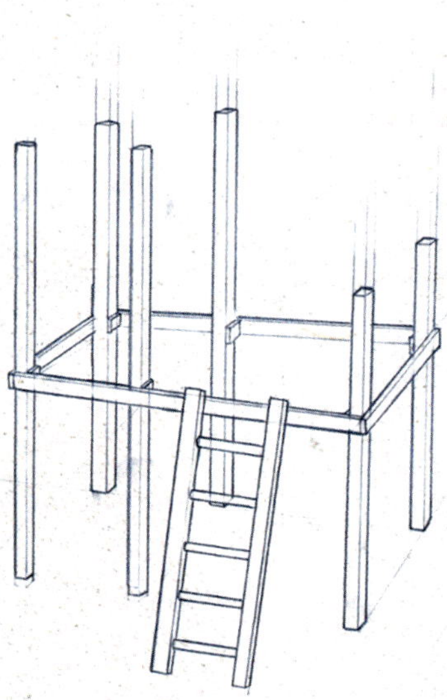

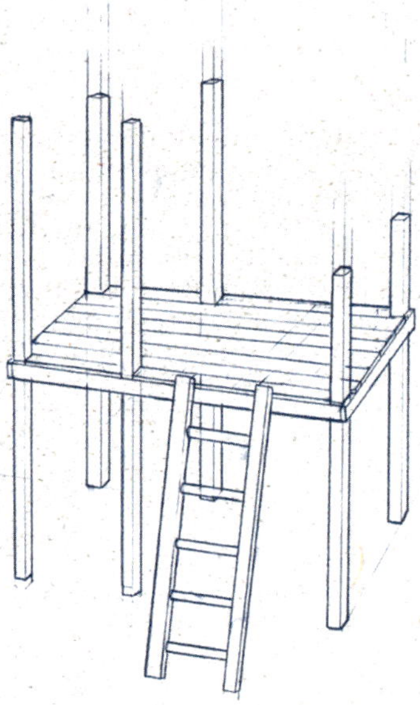

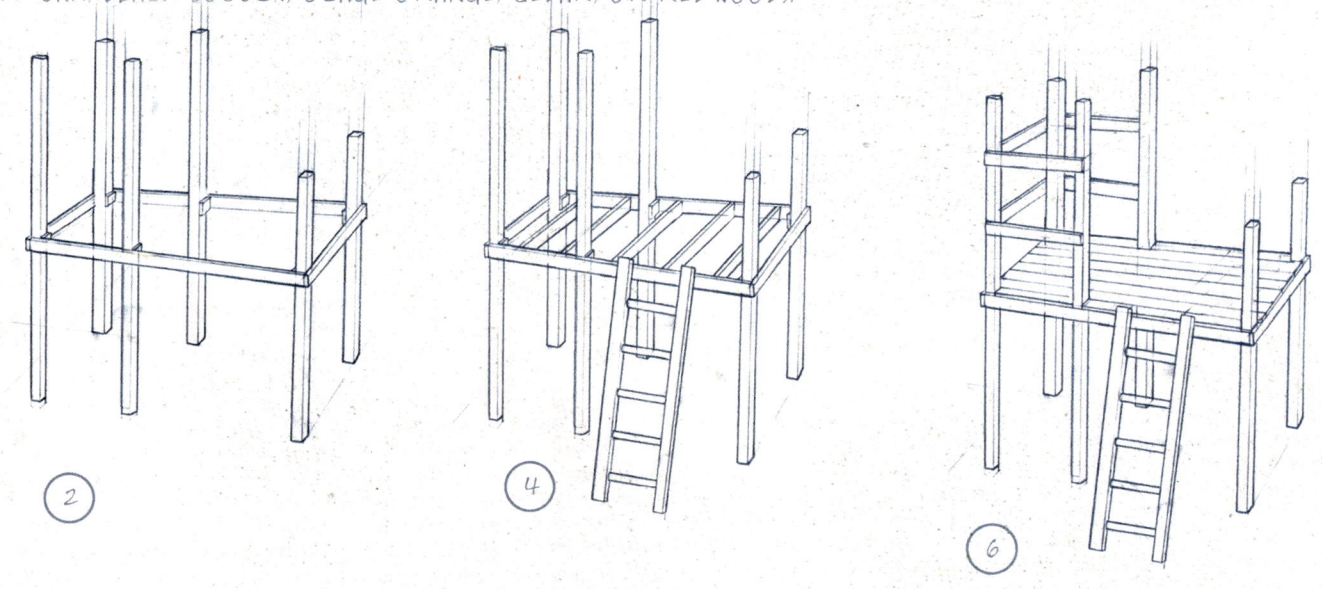

POSTS SHOULD BE AT LEAST 24" IN THE GROUND AND SET IN CEMENT FOR STABILITY. THEY ARE THE ONLY PARTS THAT NEED TO BE BUILT OF DURABLE LUMBER (EITHER TREATED OR A ROT RESISTANT SPECIES, SUCH AS WHITE OAK, BLACK LOCUST, OSAGE ORANGE, CEDAR, OR REDWOOD).

YOU'LL FIND THAT ONE OF THE GREAT THINGS ABOUT HAVING YOUR OWN SAWMILL IS THAT YOU CAN MILL WHATEVER YOU NEED AND PUT IT UP AS YOU CUT IT   OFTEN IN LESS TIME THAN IT WOULD TAKE TO GO TO THE LUMBER YARD AND BUY BOARDS THAT SEEM TO GET SMALLER AND MORE CROOKED EVERY TIME YOU BUY THEM.

NORWOOD

PROJECT #4: Trestle Table

A project like this can easily become a family heirloom.

It's not an exaggeration to say, "*They aren't building them like this anymore.*"

Well, **THEY** might not be, but **YOU** certainly can!

The trestle table is a traditional design that allows you to use air dry lumber instead of kiln dry.

The table top is a perfect use for those wide slabs, though you may need to let them air dry for several years unless you put them in a kiln.

One of the advantages of a trestle table is that it is easy to take apart for moving.

If you want a bigger challenge, try building the traditional way with mortise joints held together with a tapered peg.

Woodworkers have used mortise joints for thousands of years to join pieces of wood. It worked great then, and it still works great today. It is one of the most appealing woodwork joints, because of its strong, flush fit.

As the wood shrinks, just tap the peg in a little, and it tightens right up. You can tap the peg out to disassemble the table.

There are also a variety of design options for the base of the table.

If you bolt everything together, you can even change the base as you develop more skills as a woodworker.

This design uses a double-trestle with half-lap joints.

If you use carriage bolts to attach them to the legs, you will be able to tighten them as necessary.

The table top is 1-¾" thick and may weigh as much as 100 pounds, depending on the species of wood.

Few woodworkers ever have the opportunity to work with the kind of wide boards you can produce with your mill. Book-matched, natural "live" edge boards can make the table even more beautiful and unique.

Many folks like a little bit of roughness in the wood for a rustic appearance. You can easily achieve this by just giving the wood a light sanding instead of putting it through a planer.

As for dimensions, the common height for tables is 29".

This trestle table is 35" wide and 6' long, but you can adjust the dimensions to whatever works best for you.

You can even make narrower, scaled-down versions of this design for benches or coffee tables.

Timeless TRESTLE TABLE

THE TRESTLE TABLE IS AN OLD FASHIONED DESIGN THAT ALLOWS YOU TO USE AIR DRY LUMBER INSTEAD OF KILN DRY. THE TABLE TOP IS A PERFECT USE FOR THOSE WIDE SLABS, THOUGH YOU MAY NEED TO LET THEM AIR DRY FOR SEVERAL YEARS, UNLESS YOU PUT THEM IN A KILN. ONE OF THE ADVANTAGES OF A TRESTLE TABLE IS THAT IT IS EASY TO TAKE APART FOR MOVING. IF YOU WANT A CHALLENGE, TRY BUILDING THE TRADITIONAL WAY WITH MORTISES JOINTS HELD TOGETHER WITH A TAPERED PEG. AS THE WOOD SHRINKS, JUST TAP THE PEG IN A LITTLE, AND IT TIGHTENS RIGHT UP. OR TAP THE PEG OUT TO DISASSEMBLE THE TABLE.

THERE ARE ALSO A LOT OF DESIGN OPTIONS WITH THE BASE OF THE TABLE. IF YOU BOLT EVERYTHING TOGETHER, YOU CAN EVEN CHANGE THE BASE AS YOU DEVELOP MORE SKILLS AS A WOODWORKER.

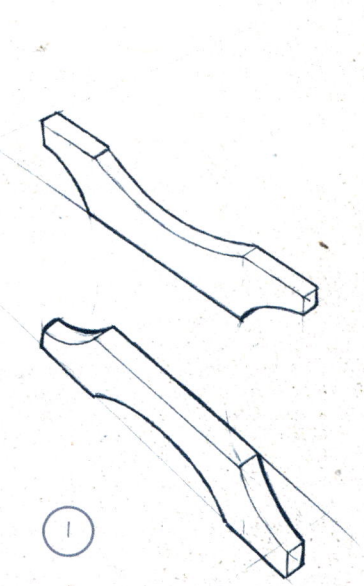

①

THE DESIGN SHOWN USES A DOUBLE TRESTLE WITH HALF LAP JOINTS. IF YOU USE CARRIAGE BOLTS TO ATTACH THEM TO YOUR LEGS, YOU WILL BE ABLE TO TIGHTEN THEM AS NECESSARY. THE TABLE TOP IS 1 3/4" THICK, AND MAY WEIGH 100 POUNDS.

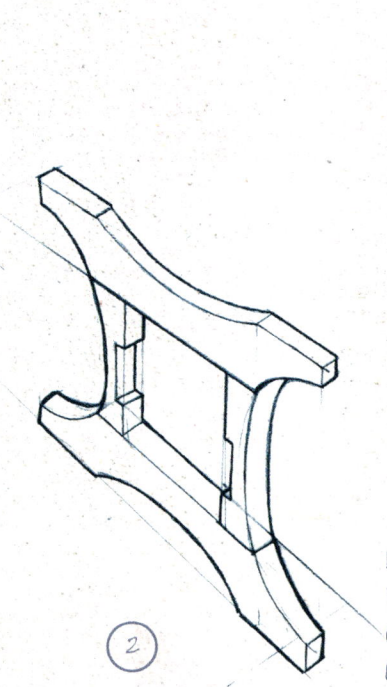

②

DEPENDING ON THE SPECIES OF WOOD, FEW WOODWORKERS EVER HAVE THE OPPORTUNITY TO WORK WITH WIDE BOARDS THAT YOU CAN PRODUCE WITH YOUR MILL AND BOOKMATCHED NATURAL "LIVE" EDGE BOARDS CAN MAKE THE TABLE EVEN MORE UNIQUE.

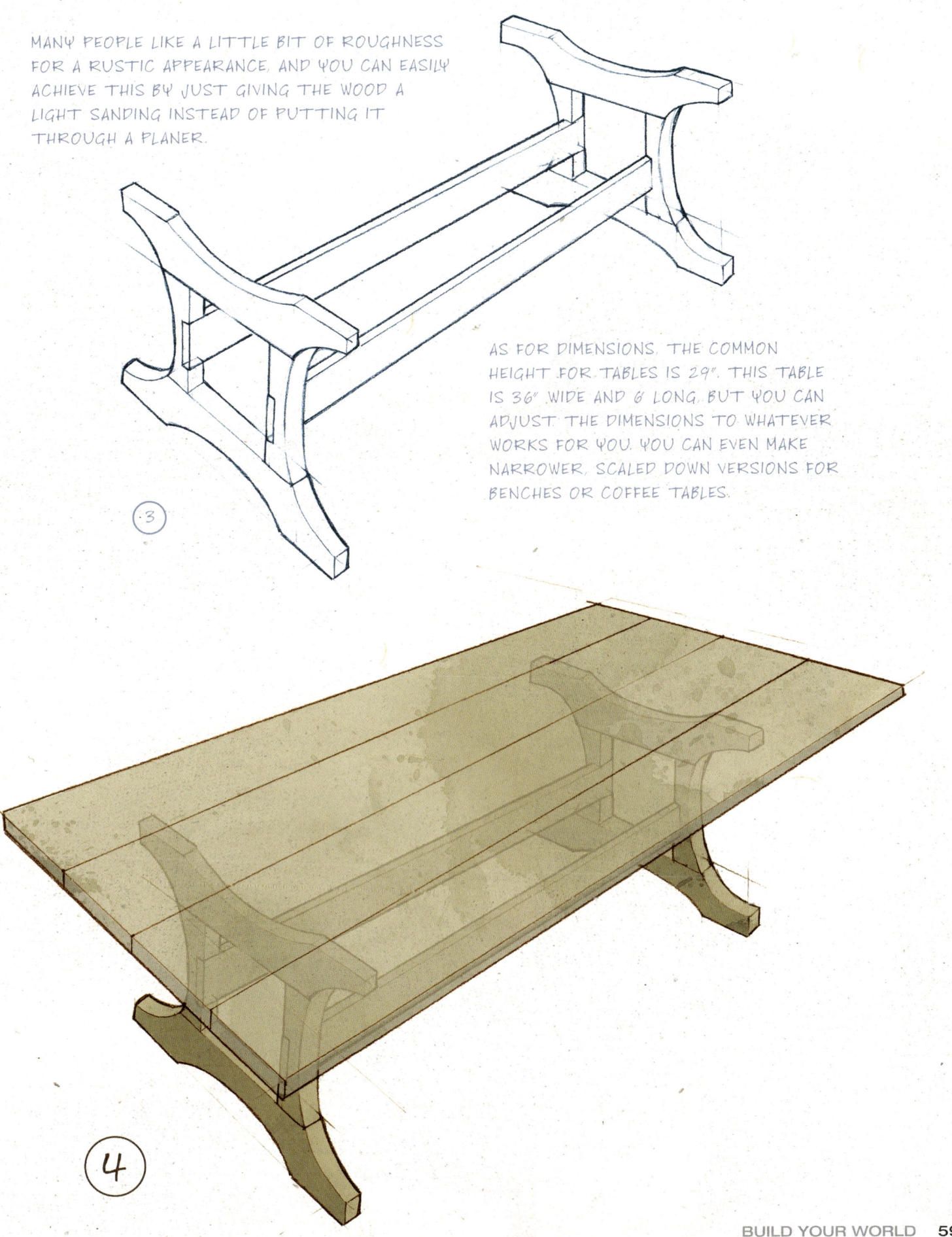

MANY PEOPLE LIKE A LITTLE BIT OF ROUGHNESS
FOR A RUSTIC APPEARANCE, AND YOU CAN EASILY
ACHIEVE THIS BY JUST GIVING THE WOOD A
LIGHT SANDING INSTEAD OF PUTTING IT
THROUGH A PLANER.

3

AS FOR DIMENSIONS, THE COMMON
HEIGHT FOR TABLES IS 29". THIS TABLE
IS 36" WIDE AND 6' LONG, BUT YOU CAN
ADJUST THE DIMENSIONS TO WHATEVER
WORKS FOR YOU. YOU CAN EVEN MAKE
NARROWER, SCALED DOWN VERSIONS FOR
BENCHES OR COFFEE TABLES.

4

These ideas are just a glimpse of all that is possible for you when you use your portable sawmill to "build your world."

The sky really is the limit when it comes to the various ways you can add more originality, quality, and beauty to your life.

Now feast your eyes on these additional examples of what Norwood sawmill owners have built with their own two hands.

Most of them started out as beginners and simply dove right in, perfecting their skills while making the sawdust fly.

Take a look at what's possible, and consider what YOU can accomplish with your portable sawmill!

The concept plans and designs in this chapter, and throughout this book, are included solely for inspiration. They are not official plans, designs or drawings created or approved by any engineers or architects. They should not be used as actual plans or drawings upon which to base construction. Have all actual plans and drawings created and/or reviewed by a local architect, structural engineer, and/or certified general contractor to verify compliance to local codes, snow loading, seismic and soil conditions, energy requirements, and all other regulations prior to commencing construction. Norwood Industries Inc. and Norwood Sawmills USA Inc. will not be held liable for any damages whatsoever resulting from the use of any of the concept plans and drawings.

First Log –
Let The Sawdust Fly!

4

At this point, you have a comprehensive overview of what to be aware of when choosing your personal sawmill, and have discovered some intriguing possibilities for making money with your sawmill.

In addition, it's possible you already have visions of "building your world" running through your mind too.

By now it should be pretty obvious that the level you can take your milling to is only limited by your imagination and willingness to get in there and DO it!

If you're serious about being a skilled sawyer, now it's time to get down and dirty with some important aspects of the fascinating world of turning a variety of rough logs into all kinds of beautiful lumber like this…

Yep, if you're like most sawmill owners, you really do think it's beautiful! And being able to do this with your own two hands is definitely satisfying too.

So let's take the next steps together, about what to expect with that first log.

First of all, if you're ready to become the proud owner of a portable sawmill or already have one, congratulations on becoming a "Doer" instead of a dreamer.

A lot of folks spend their entire lives wishing, hoping, and dreaming instead of taking decisive action. And quite frankly, life is far too short for that.

Hal Dougherty Don't wait till you retire! I see so many people who say they want to get a sawmill for their retirement years… Don't wait! Go ahead and get one. I'm 65 and I got a manual mill to save money and also because I sell products, not lumber and I don't saw for other people. Made into gunstocks (my main product), I get $40/bft for my lumber! Don't wait til you are too old to get the most use out of your equipment. Get your own sawmill and you can make and sell yard barns, rustic slab benches, rocking horses, moldings. If I'd been able to own a sawmill and enough woodworking equipment to get started, I'd be rich today. I'm 65 and I wish I'd made the plunge years ago. Here's one of my gunstocks and one of my rustic benches. The stock is laminated cherry & walnut and the bench is beautiful figured maple.

Unlike · Reply · 👍 3 · July 6 at 8:07am

There's no question, the arrival of your portable sawmill is exciting. Your creative juices are going to be pumping on overtime! So let's prime the pump by…

Celebrating Your First Log!

Once you've got your mill set up and ready to mill your first log, you have reached a milestone in your career as a sawyer.

Before your first cut you will:

✓ **Level the mill...**

✓ **Put on a new blade...**

✓ **Set the tension...**

✓ **Adjust the tracking...**

✓ **Align the guides...**

✓ **Line the mill up with the crossbunks...**

✓ **Fill the gas tank...**

✓ **Fill the water tank...**

✓ **Check the oil...**

✓ **Now you're ready!**

Remember, your first log will be a learning experience.

So start out with a low-value log, but one that is fairly straight and small enough you can handle it easily.

An eight-foot log around 14" in diameter would be ideal.

So what should you do with it besides push it through your sawmill?

For starters, you will need a way to store and dry the wood you mill.

So a great idea is to start out milling some 6" x 6" beams to stack the wood on, and some 1" x 1" called **stickers**.

Stickers are spacers that go between the layers of wood to allow air circulation through the stack as it dries.

After milling, you can cut them in half to get 4' wide stacks, something like this…

As you build up your inventory of lumber, you'll find you never have enough blocks and stickers, so you might as well start out by cutting your first three logs for this purpose.

Now that you know WHAT to cut, the next question is HOW to cut it.

The First Cut:

If the log has much taper to it, setting it on the sawmill with the small end toward the start of the cut makes it easier to figure out where to make the first cut.

This is not a hard and fast rule though. You will eventually learn to mill the log from either end.

With the log in place and firmly clamped down, it is time to map out what it will become. For now, that will be your blocks and stickers.

The idea is to square the log into a "cant." Basically, a cant is a partially sawn log with at least one flat side.

When you square the log into a cant, you then remove the boards from each side until you wind up with the 6" x 6" in the centre. If possible, it is best to have the growth rings centered in the 6" x 6" block, so it will be less likely to warp as it dries.

This is not critical for this blocking, but it is a good skill to learn. All of the "side lumber" will be 7/8" wide, and you will later cut it to square to make stickers.

Note that mud and grit will quickly dull a blade, so check the log along the path the blade will take when it cuts.

If you see mud or grit where the blade will ENTER the log, you can either remove it (a hatchet works well for this) or turn the log so the blade enters into clean wood.

The first cut that removes the top of the log is called a "slabbing" cut.

- **Start the cut with the blade about an inch below the top of the log.**

- **Take a deep breath, bring the engine up to full throttle, and ease the blade into the log.**

You probably won't even be able to feel when the blade starts cutting. It will be a little like pushing a shopping cart (but without the irritating wobbly wheel!).

When the blade exits the other end of the log, remove the slab and take a good look at the cut.

It should be straight and have fine saw marks in it.

Now take a minute to BREATHE and smile a lot. You have begun! ☺

Turning the Log:

Most sawyers turn the log 90 degrees after the first cut, so the flat cut rests against the log stops.

Make sure the log stops are below the cutting line before you clamp the log down.

On most mills, there is nothing to prevent you from cutting into the log stops and ruining a blade. It's possible you will eventually do this, but there's no need to do it on your first log!

The preferred tool for handling logs is a **cant hook**. It allows you to hook onto the log, giving you good leverage to rotate the log. It may seem awkward at first, but after a while, using it will become second nature.

The second slab cuts much like the first.

The third and fourth slabbing cuts should start on an even inch mark, since you want a 6" x 6" out of the centre, and you will be lowering the blade 1" after each cut.

After you have cut the fourth slab, you have a cant and are ready to start making boards!

Doug Skaggs ▶ **Norwood Portable Sawmills**
March 9 · 🌎

Safe to say; a perfect square. Love this mill!!

Like · Comment   Share   · 👍 13 ↪ 11

Simply cut down in 1" increments until you are about 3" from the center of the log.

Then turn the log 90 degrees and repeat.

When you cut boards on the 3rd and 4th sides of the cant, stop at the 6" mark.

You should wind up with a 6" x 6" cant, and a number of boards of various widths.

Evaluating Your Cut:

Before you take the 6" x 6" beam off the mill, check it for square and accuracy.

The ends should be perfectly square, and each side should be exactly 6" wide.

If the sides are not square, adjust the log stops so they are perpendicular to the crossbunks.

If the dimension is off, adjust the scale to match the distance between the top of the crossbunks and the bottom of the blade.

Stickers:

You now have a square cant and boards of varying widths.

To cut the stickers, put the boards back on the mill edgewise. Four at a time is enough for starters.

Pay close attention to the position of the log stops as you cut the strips.

You'll want the stops high enough to support the boards, but be sure to stop cutting before the blade is low enough to hit them.

Then turn the board over so the flat edges are against the bunks, lower the stops, and finish off the strips.

Leave the last strips 2" wide so that you don't have to cut too close to the stops and clamps.

Most lumber piles are about 4' wide, so you'll want to cut the blocks and stickers into 4' lengths.

More Logs:

Congratulations and high fives! Now you're a sawyer.

Pile the slabs a convenient distance from your mill. Maybe you'll use them for firewood next winter. Cut the next three logs about the same as you did the first one.

The blocks and stickers should be about 20" apart when you stack the logs on them for drying, so you'll need:

- **6 blocks to support a pile of 8' logs...**

- **7 blocks for 10' logs...**

- **9 blocks for 12' logs...**

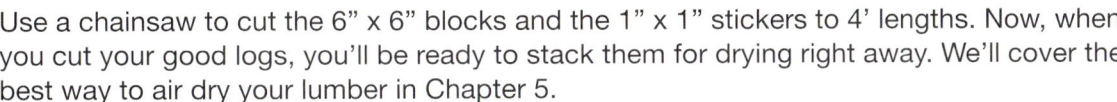

Use a chainsaw to cut the 6" x 6" blocks and the 1" x 1" stickers to 4' lengths. Now, when you cut your good logs, you'll be ready to stack them for drying right away. We'll cover the best way to air dry your lumber in Chapter 5.

End of the Day:

Most manufacturers recommend loosening the blade when you stop cutting for the day. If you don't have the mill in a shed or a carriage cover, throw a tarp over the head rig.

Then shake the sawdust out of your pockets, and call it a day!

Drying Your Wood

Perhaps you think once you begin sawing logs into lumber, that's all there is to it.

However, there's more to it than that.

You have a lot invested in your logs. And you don't want to see your investment turn into a very expensive pile of deluxe firewood.

Without proper care, this is exactly what will happen.

The good news is…

Drying Wood Isn't Difficult!

But it does take a little planning, and a good chunk of time.

If you've ever been to a lumberyard and spent time sorting through all the warped, twisted, and cracked boards, you've seen firsthand the results of poor drying technique.

If you have purchased a portable sawmill, or are planning to do so in the near future, you very likely want to have quality lumber to build with, sell, or both.

The problem is, wood shrinks when it dries.

To get a better idea of how this works, do this simple experiment.

Saturate a sponge with water, and note the size.

Then squeeze the water out.

Even if you have Herculean strength, no matter how hard you squeeze, the sponge will stay the same size. This is because it still has some moisture bound up in the cell walls.

The only way to get rid of this moisture is to let the sponge finish drying by evaporation.

If the sponge gets airflow all around it, it will shrink, but maintain its shape.

But if you place the sponge on a flat surface, it will curl, because the moisture on the top evaporates more quickly than on the bottom.

You've probably accidentally seen this experiment play out in your kitchen sink!

Wood does exactly the same thing.

So unless you want your precious wood to end up looking like a curled up sponge, you need to have an effective way to dry it evenly and slowly.

Stickers, stickers, and more stickers!

Proper Drying of Wood Needs to Begin as Soon as you Cut the Tree!

✓ SEAL THE DEAL

Moisture moving out the ends of the board can cause cracks known as "end checking". To avoid this, apply a sealant to the ends of the log as soon as it has been cut.

The best sealant is a product called AnchorSeal.

This is a wax that seals the end of the log and does not leave a residue on the wood. It can also be applied to the ends of boards after they have been milled, but it is best to apply it as soon as possible when you cut the log.

Latex paint of any color is another option, though it is not as effective as AnchorSeal.

The real key to drying is properly stacking the lumber after milling.

✓ LET THE DRYING BEGIN

The boards should go straight from the mill to the drying rack.

This is especially important in the summer when decay takes place quickly. Fungus can be noticeable in the boards even after just one day if they are "dead stacked" without stickers between the rows for air circulation.

This means you need both a place to dry the wood, as well as the blocking and stickers *before* you cut the first board.

Your drying yard should be in a level, open area with good air circulation.

The 6" x 6" blocks should be about 4' long and spaced no more than 24" apart for 1" thick boards.

You can make sure it is flat by pulling a string diagonally across the blocks, or by sighting down them.

Shim the 6" x 6" blocking if necessary. Any twist or dip in the pile will result in warped boards.

✓ STICKERS, STICKERS, AND MORE STICKERS!

It takes a lot of stickers to dry lumber!

If you have 1,000 board feet of 1" thick by 10' long boards, you will need enough stickers for 25 layers of wood, six stickers per layer, or...150 stickers!

See what I mean?

You may cut some as you go, but get on board with the fact that you can never have too many stickers.

Lumber
JACK SAYS

"*Any time you have a log that will not make quality lumber, consider cutting it into blocking and stickers.*"

Board Thickness Considerations

Another consideration for drying is the thickness of the boards themselves.

It may be tempting to cut a variety of board thicknesses, but this only leads to headaches when drying the wood.

Each layer of boards needs to be the same thickness, or the stacks will be uneven.

Stick with standard thicknesses, such as boards that are:

- **4/4 (1" thick)**

- **6/4 (1-1/2" thick)**

- **8/4 (2" thick)**

They will be easier to sort and dry, and easier to sell later.

A slight gap between boards to allow better air circulation is also a good idea.

Set your poorest boards aside to form the bottom row of the pile.

They will act as a moisture barrier between the ground and your better lumber.

As you stack the lumber, make sure the stickers are arranged in a vertical column, each directly above the one below it.

That way, they transfer the weight of the pile straight down to the blocking without putting stress on the boards.

The dimensions of the stack depends on several factors...

- **How high can you reach?**

- **If you pick up your pile with a fork truck, how much weight can it handle?**

- **Will you be using a kiln for drying?**

If you will be loading the boards into a kiln, it is much easier to stack it for air-drying to a size that will easily fit in the kiln. Otherwise you may have to handle it twice.

To help hold the wood flat, many people put weights on their wood.

Concrete blocks are a favorite, but another easy method is barrels of water.

You can put empty barrels on top of the stack, then pump them full of water for weight.

You can then siphon the water out of the barrels when you are ready to unstack the lumber.

Finally, cover the stack to protect it from the elements.

Metal roofing works well. But a tarp is fine if it covers the top of the stack and doesn't interfere with the airflow through the sides.

Then comes the hard part.

Waiting...

The rule of thumb is to allow one year of air-drying per inch of thickness of the board. But this depends on species and location.

For example, sycamore dries more quickly than white oak. And lumber air dries more quickly in Phoenix, Arizona than in Seattle, Washington.

Generally, wood is considered to be air dried once the moisture content of the wood reaches around 18%.

A good moisture meter is an important tool.

Be sure to measure the moisture content of several pieces throughout the stack, even though this means unstacking some of the wood.

Air-dry wood is suitable for outdoor applications such as outdoor furniture and porch decking.

Wood to be used indoors will eventually dry to around 8% moisture content.

Once brought indoors, it will continue to dry and shrink, no matter how long it has air-dried.

The early craftsmen developed ingenious techniques such as trestle tables and frame & panel cabinets to allow air-dry wood to shrink without cracking or warping.

Whether used indoors or out, the moisture content of wood will equalize into the average relative humidity in the air.

The Benefits of Kiln Drying

Kiln drying increases the value of wood in two ways.

✓ **1. It quickly brings the wood to a moisture content that matches an indoor environment. In other words, it's FASTER.**

✓ **2. It kills any insects or fungus in the wood.**

Kiln drying adds to the cost of processing the wood but, in general, the added value outweighs the cost of kiln drying because the wood is bug free and ready to use much sooner.

You can cut the cost of kiln drying wood by air drying it first, but the down side of pre-drying the wood is that it will be up to a year before it is ready to use.

If you are impatient, the wood can go straight from the sawmill to the kiln.

The time required to kiln dry the wood depends on the kiln design, and wood thickness. **But one to two weeks is typical.** Much better than a year!

Here's a smart idea for an economical way to kiln dry your wood…

A Solar Kiln

There are several advantages to using a solar kiln.

- **It is relatively inexpensive**

- **You can build it yourself**

- **On sunny days, a well-designed solar kiln will be as much as 30 degrees hotter than the outside air temperature**

- **Your wood is protected from the elements**

- **It's much faster**

Here is a simple plan you can use to build yourself a solar kiln (see pages 84-85):

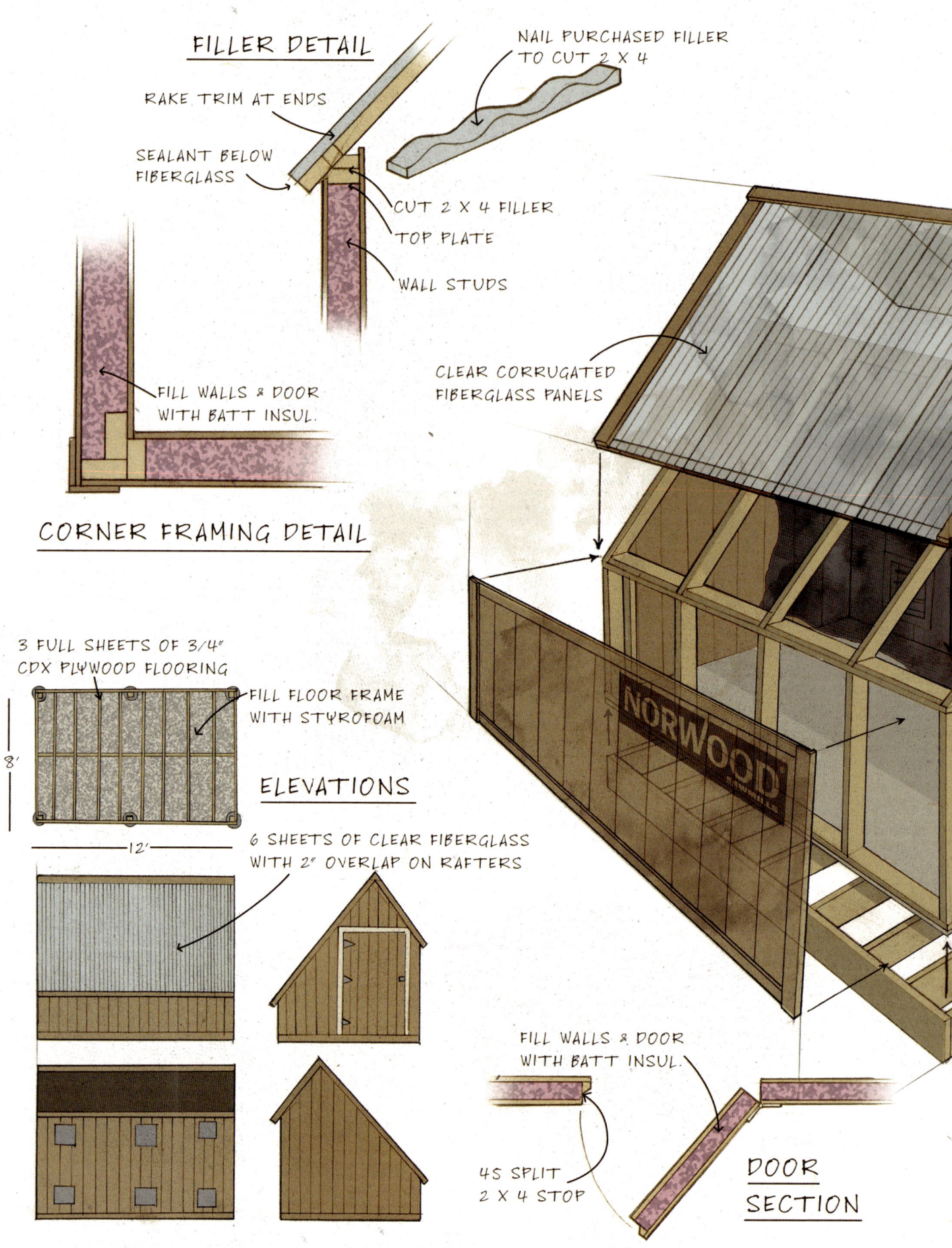

FILLER DETAIL

NAIL PURCHASED FILLER
TO CUT 2 X 4

RAKE TRIM AT ENDS

SEALANT BELOW
FIBERGLASS

CUT 2 X 4 FILLER
TOP PLATE
WALL STUDS

FILL WALLS & DOOR
WITH BATT INSUL.

CORNER FRAMING DETAIL

CLEAR CORRUGATED
FIBERGLASS PANELS

3 FULL SHEETS OF 3/4"
CDX PLYWOOD FLOORING

FILL FLOOR FRAME
WITH STYROFOAM

8'

12'

ELEVATIONS

6 SHEETS OF CLEAR FIBERGLASS
WITH 2" OVERLAP ON RAFTERS

NORWOOD

FILL WALLS & DOOR
WITH BATT INSUL.

45 SPLIT
2 X 4 STOP

DOOR
SECTION

SOLAR KILN

NORWOOD SAWMILLS

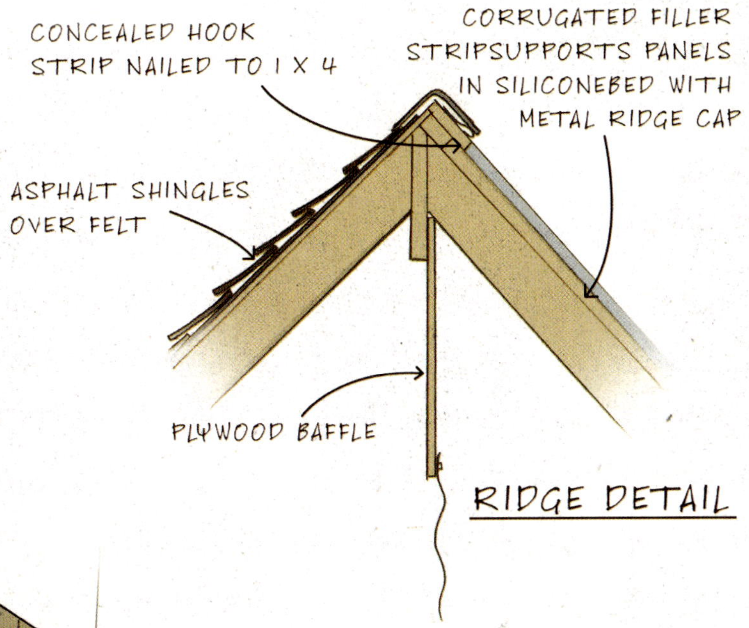

CONCEALED HOOK
STRIP NAILED TO 1 X 4

CORRUGATED FILLER
STRIPSUPPORTS PANELS
IN SILICONEBED WITH
METAL RIDGE CAP

ASPHALT SHINGLES
OVER FELT

METAL DRIP
EDGE

PLYWOOD BAFFLE

RIDGE DETAIL

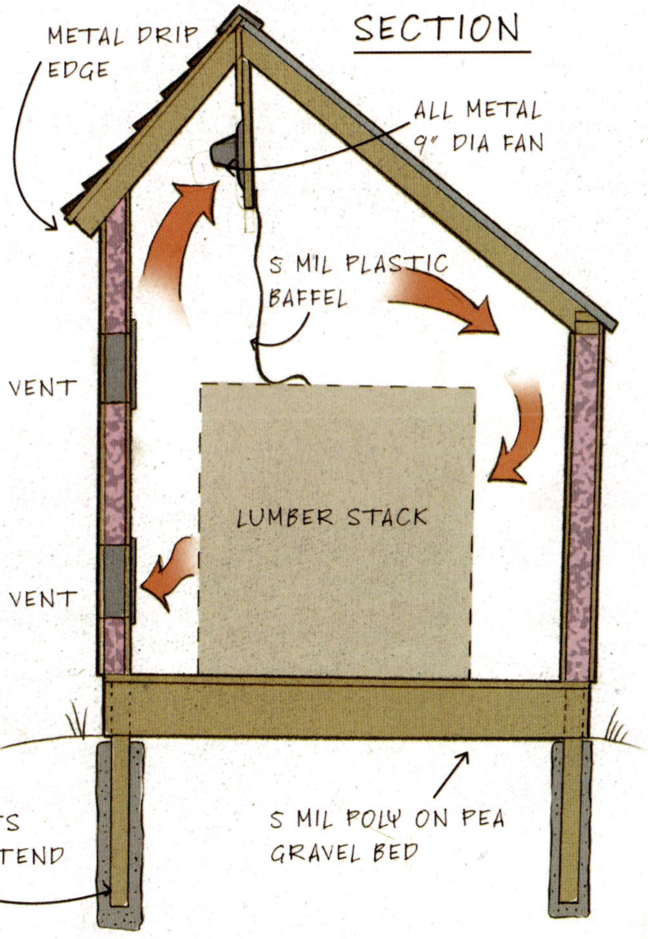

METAL DRIP
EDGE

SECTION

ALL METAL
9" DIA FAN

5 MIL PLASTIC
BAFFEL

VENT

LUMBER STACK

VENT

3/4" T.1.11
TEXTURED PLYWOOD
SIDING

4 X 4 TREATED POSTS
SET IN CONCRETE EXTEND
TO FROST LINE

5 MIL POLY ON PEA
GRAVEL BED

There's another reason for careful consideration of wood drying procedures…

Building Your Sawmill Business

If you're considering turning your portable sawmill into a thriving business with a solid customer base, wood drying is how you can create an army of happy clients.

You want to make your customer as successful in what they're trying to do as you possibly can.

Often, **the weakest link in a sawmilling business is failure to plan for the proper drying and storing of their wood.**

Serving your customer well goes beyond the obvious cutting of the lumber. In far too many instances, once the lumber is cut, the customer thinks everything is fine if the wood is piled up neatly.

But as you've learned today, **if you don't properly air-dry it, their wood will rot and warp and otherwise become unusable.**

And that sours the whole experience for them and does nothing positive for your business.

Here's How to Handle Wood Drying for Your Customers

During your initial contact with a customer, take a few minutes to discuss the importance of drying the lumber. Find out how they're going to use the wood.

It is practically guaranteed that your average customer will not have thought about the proper drying of their wood, or even be aware of why it is important.

But after you have a conversation with them, their awareness will be dramatically increased.

Then work with them to make sure to cut the necessary blocks and stickers.

You can let them know…

"OK, we need some 6" x 6" blocking, and we need to cut stickers to use as spacers between the layers of wood, so it dries properly for you."

Not only will your customers undoubtedly be impressed with your expertise and attention to detail on their behalf, they'll appreciate it when they end up with straight, quality lumber that exceeds their expectations.

This is probably the single biggest service other than the milling itself you can provide. And it's a sure fire way to get referrals and repeat business too!

6

Maximize Your Sawing Pattern Potential

There are a number of different sawing patterns that will become important to you as you gain expertise with your portable sawmill.

Different sawing patterns are suitable for different types of woodworking. The sawing pattern determines the final value of the lumber, and how it will be used.

Each pattern is created by how you orient and cut the log on your portable sawmill.

Lumber cut from logs typically is cut in one of these three ways:

Plain (Flat) Sawn

Plain sawn produces the least expensive and most common lumber.

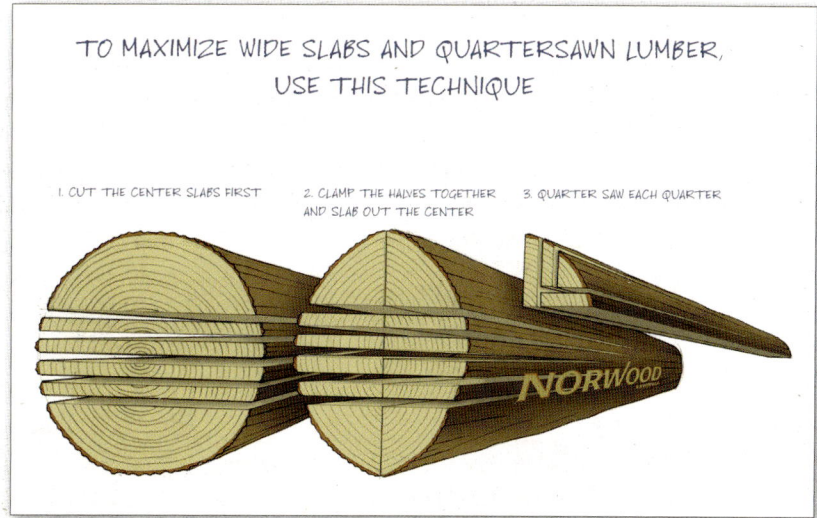

TO MAXIMIZE WIDE SLABS AND QUARTERSAWN LUMBER, USE THIS TECHNIQUE

1. CUT THE CENTER SLABS FIRST   2. CLAMP THE HALVES TOGETHER AND SLAB OUT THE CENTER   3. QUARTER SAW EACH QUARTER

Quarter Sawn

Quarter sawn creates some beautiful grain patterns that can enhance the design of what you are building.

It is also more expensive, and more valuable, than plain sawn lumber.

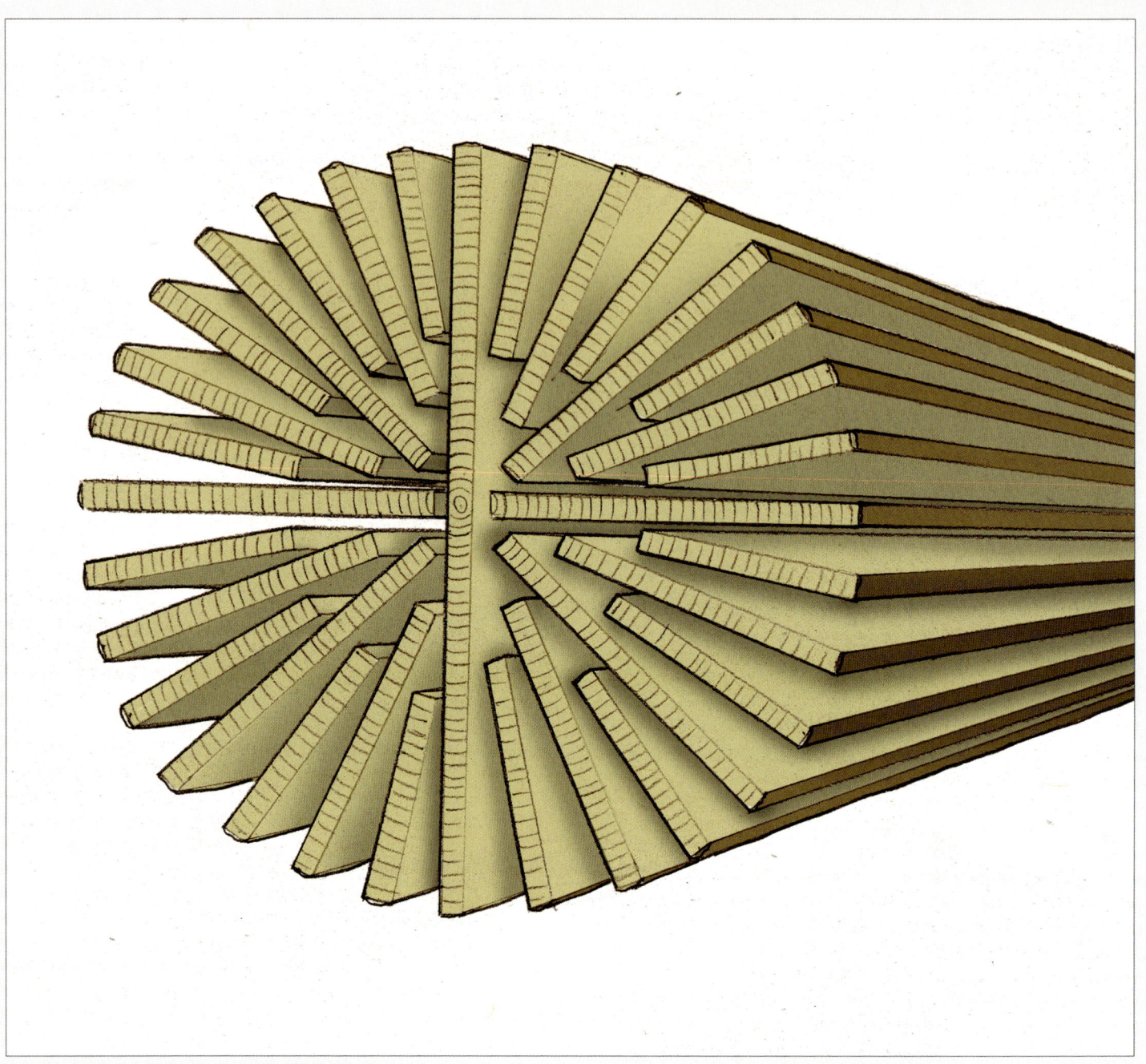

Rift Sawn

Rift sawn is the most expensive sawing pattern because it produces the most waste. This is also one of the reasons it is the least common.

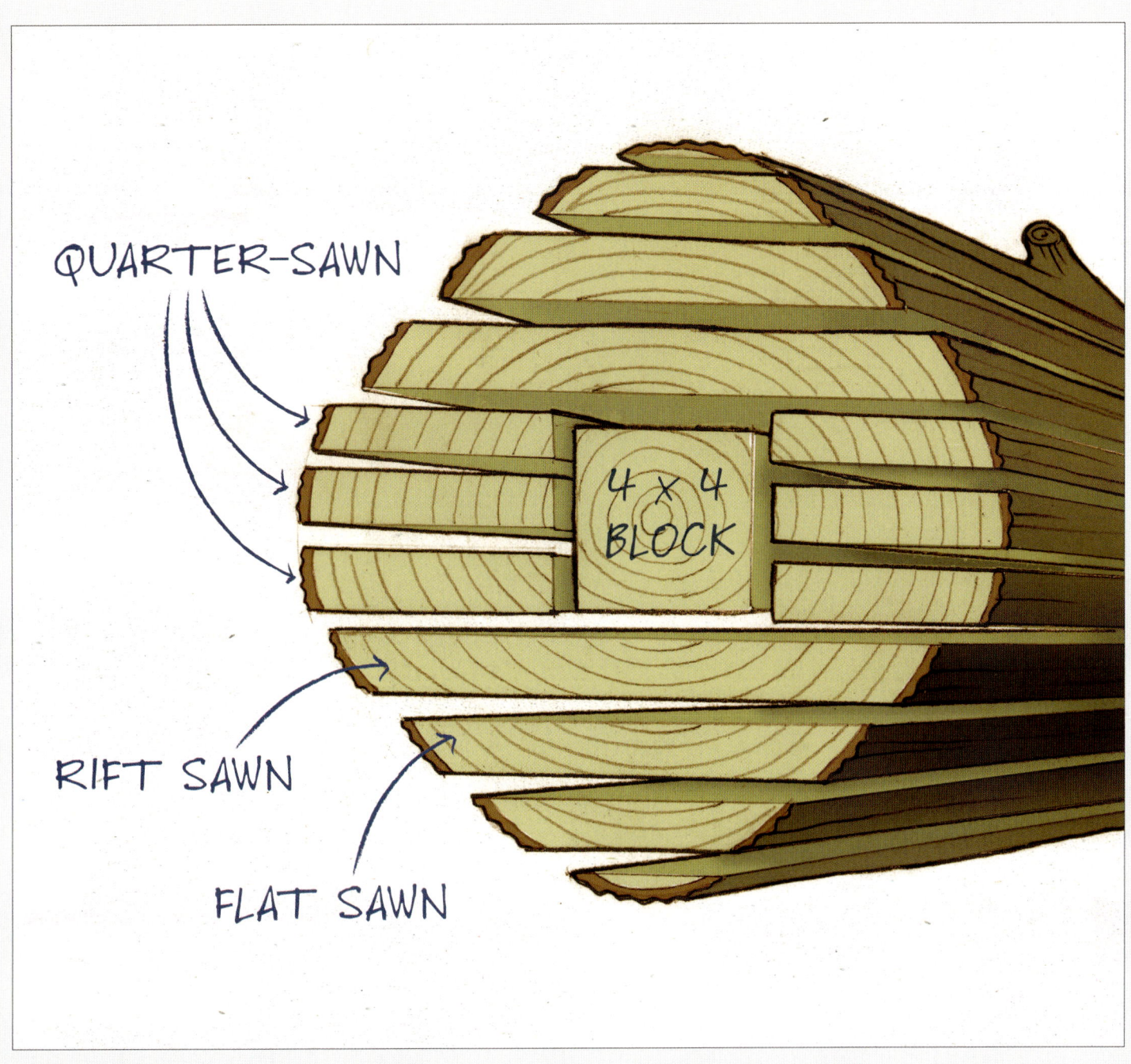

QUARTER-SAWN

4 x 4
BLOCK

RIFT SAWN

FLAT SAWN

Quarter, rift, and **plain sawn** boards each show their own particular patterns.

Another less common cutting style is called **Slabbing**. Slabbing creates natural edges that may appeal to woodworkers who build rustic or natural form furniture. But you need to be aware that it can push a mill to its limits on wide cuts.

In reality, most cutting jobs will require you to be able to produce a combination of different cuts. And there is a very important reason for this…

…Your Customers.

As we've discussed in a previous chapter, a great many sawmill owners find they can soon be in business, even if that was not your original intention.

And running a sawmill business means providing what the customer wants.

The ironic part of this is that, what a customer wants, may not always be what they ask for. They may not even know how to ask for what they actually want as a final outcome for their lumber.

That's where your "super-sleuthing" customer service skills come into play!

Before you make even one cut for a customer, you need to determine what the end product will be by having a conversation with them.

By asking a few key questions about what their goals are, and what they would like to achieve, you can work through the process of providing the best lumber for them.

Cutting from a Cant

You will probably find that often your customers know just enough about lumber to request quarter-sawn lumber.

Quarter-sawn lumber is the most stable, produces fancy ray flecks in oak and sycamore, and has the best acoustic properties for string instrument soundboards.

So it's easy to see why it is so popular!

Some customers may even ask for ALL quarter-sawn lumber because they want those gorgeous flecks and designs in their lumber.

While this can be done, it is not the best use of the wood, and takes more time to cut. This, in itself, is a good justification to charge by the hour.

Keep in mind, you want to serve your clients in the best way possible and not waste their money or your time in the process.

So, for example, if your customer wants quarter sawn-lumber for a beautiful table top, you may be able to mill that and then use other cuts for the legs, stretchers and braces.

Here's an example of how a project like this might go...

When discussing milling the log, one of your first questions to the customer should be *"How wide is your planer?"*

You will then mill the logs into boards that will fit through it.

• Generally, you won't cut wider than 10", unless requested to do so.

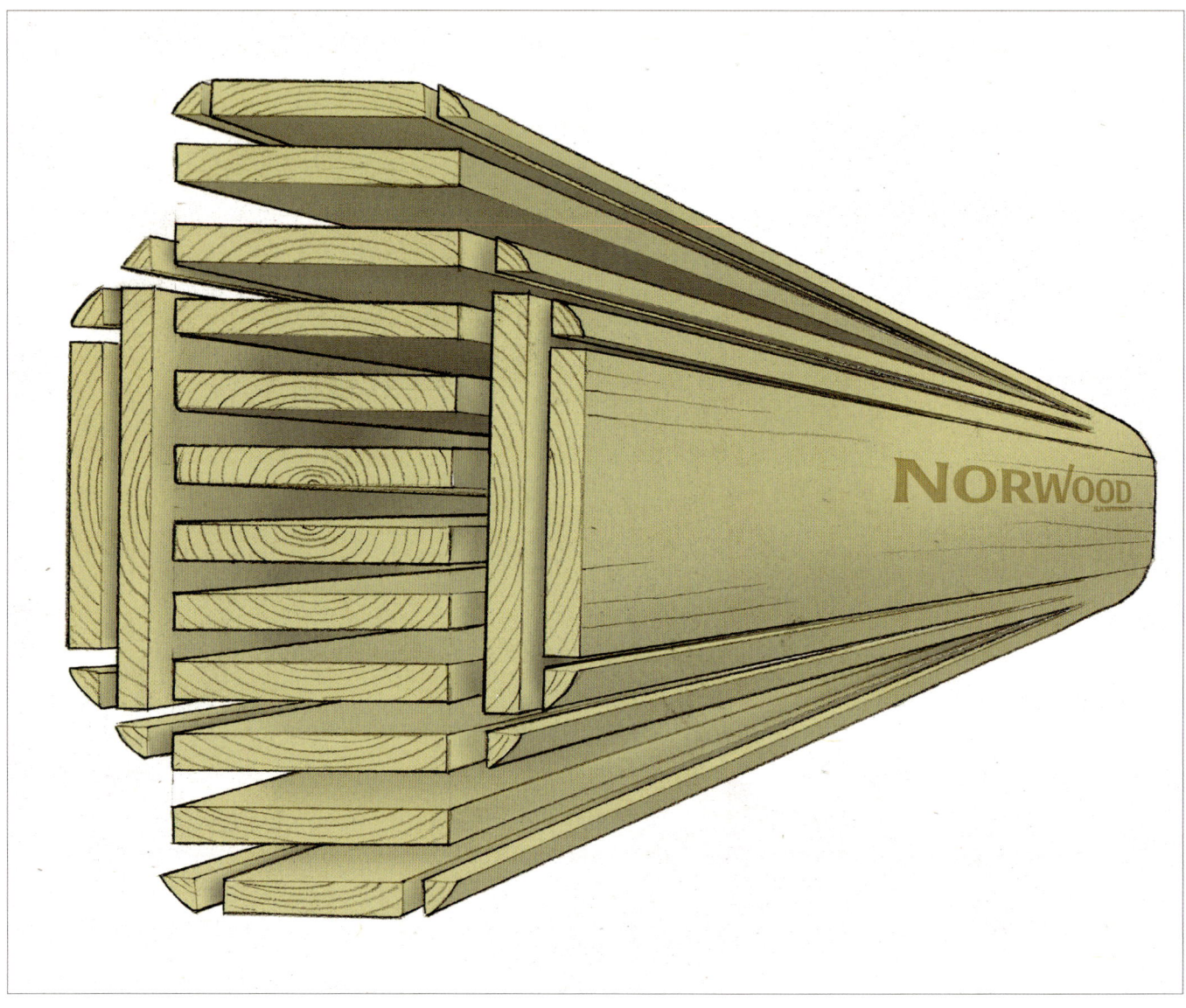

Sawing Patterns

Here is a typical sawing pattern that is efficient both in time and in use of the log.

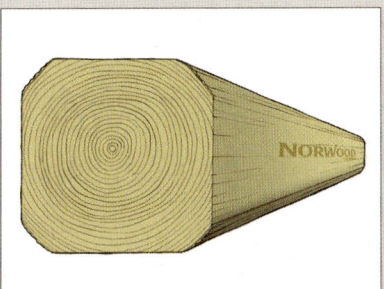

✓ Start out squaring the cant so there is a flat surface on each side.

1

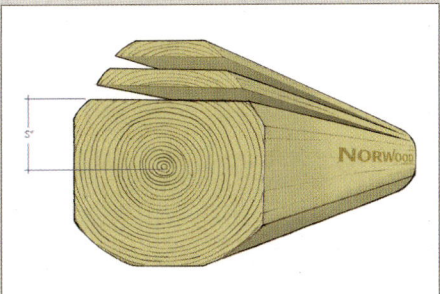

✓ Then mill boards to 5" above the center of the growth rings.

2

✓ Then rotate the cant 180 degrees and mill down to 10", which centers the growth rings in the cant.

3

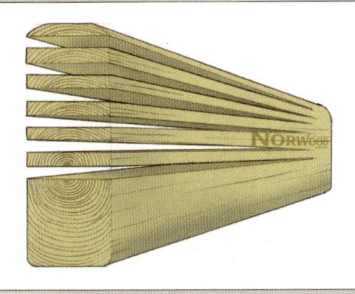

✓ Next, rotate the log 90 degrees so you saw 10" wide boards straight down through the cant.

4

✓ When you get the cant down to about 5" thick, you can use it as backing to help hold any boards that need edging.

5

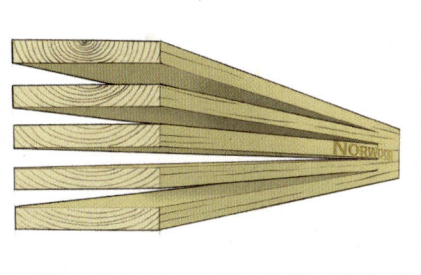

✓ When the edging is finished, rotate the cant 180 degrees and finish cutting the boards.

6

Centering the growth rings in the cant in this way keeps the boards from bowing as they dry.

Cutting like this is a little more work, but makes for a happy customer and repeat business!

Quarter-sawn lumber is also called "Vertical Grain."

Looking at the board from the end, the growth rings are almost 90 degrees to the flat side of the board.

Quarter-sawn boards are less prone to cupping as they dry, which makes them ideal for wide products like table tops.

The grain is generally straighter and does not distract from the design of the woodworking project.

Quarter-sawn oak and sycamore have ray flecks that give the wood an exotic appearance.

Builders of stringed instruments (luthiers) have considerable knowledge about the value of quarter-sawn wood for the acoustical properties, and can be very picky about the wood.

Some customers may ask you to "quarter saw" logs because they have heard it is better.

David Boyt ▶ **Norwood Portable Sawmills**
November 20 · 🌐

Quarter sawing this white oak log took a little thought and time, but the results were worth it! the clamping system on the Norwood HD36 made it a piece of cake.

The fact of the matter is, any sawing job will automatically yield 15% to 20% quarter sawn lumber without any special sawing techniques being used.

This may be enough for your customer, if they only want wood for a table top or a bench.

However, when sawing wood to sell, you will want to separate out the quarter-sawn and charge a premium for it.

The thing you need to remember is the waste of wood and additional time required usually makes quarter sawing all the boards impractical.

It is not unreasonable to double the price for quarter sawing lumber.

For those who still want to maximize the quarter-sawn lumber from their logs, this is how you do it…

There are many ways to quarter-saw wood. This technique maximizes the amount of quarter-sawn boards while making efficient use of time and material.

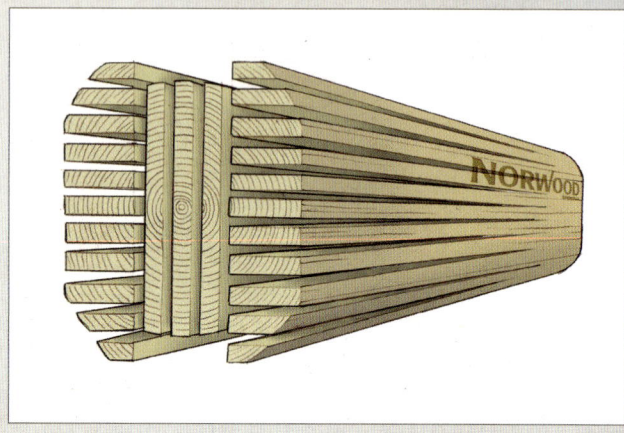

✓ **Start by cutting two or three slabs out of the center of the log.**

1

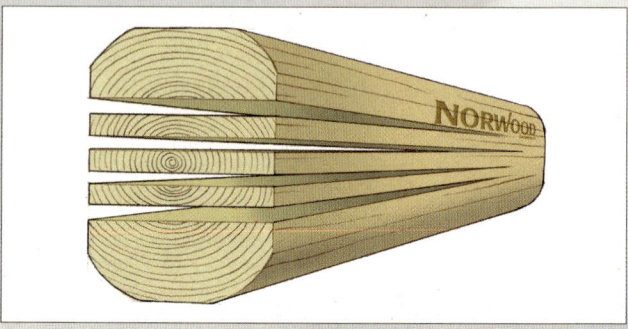

✓ **Set these slabs aside.**

✓ **Then rotate the two halves 90 degrees, clamp them together, and saw down through both of them at the same time.**

2

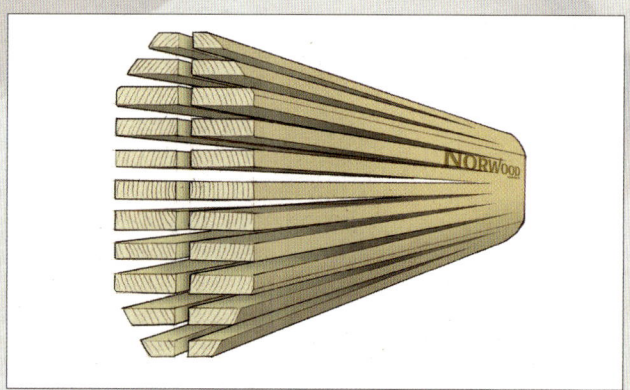

✓ **About half way through the cant, rotate it 180 degrees so that you will have a good surface to clamp to for the final cuts.**

3

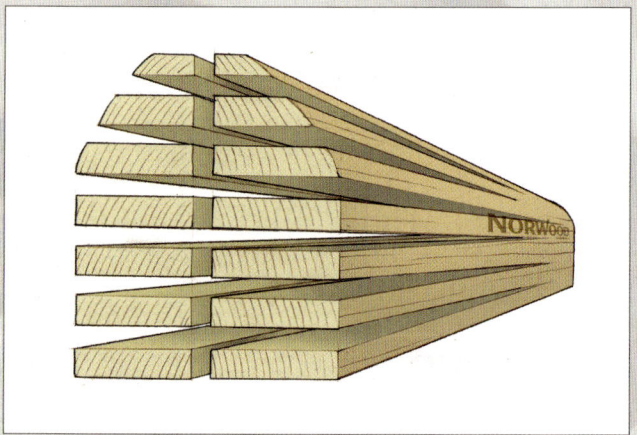

✓ **You will get more quarter sawn boards as you cut the two halves.**

4

It is possible to get even more than 50% yield, but it involves more time and effort.

It requires cutting the halves into quarters, and then individually milling each quarter and turning the quarter after each cut.

The last pieces will be small, until you get down to pieces that are too small to use. These could be used for turning blanks to make legs and spindles.

Plain or flat sawn lumber is cut from the edges of the logs.

The width of the boards is parallel to the growth rings.

It is basically cut 90 degrees to quarter sawn boards. It can have a beautiful grain, often widely separated at the center, and tighter at the edges.

Normal sawing will give you about 50% flat sawn boards.

The wood has a tendency to cup as it dries, so you may need to cut it a little thicker so the woodworker can flatten it with a planer to get the desired thickness.

Finally, you may hear of "rift sawn". This wood has an angle between the quarter and flat sawn.

Slab cutting:

Slab cutting, also called flitch cutting and live sawing, offers some interesting challenges and possibilities for both the sawyer and the woodworker.

This involves sawing boards from the log without turning it.

While it seems like this should go fairly quickly, it means that every cut goes through the grit that is typically embedded in the bark of the log. So you will find that the blade dulls more quickly. It also means you will be making wide cuts when you reach the center of the log.

If the diameter of the log exceeds the maximum width of cut of the saw, you will need to adjust your sawing strategy.

Slab sawing is very useful for crooked logs, since there is no loss of wood from cutting them into square cants.

Many woodworkers like the unique shape of slab cutting for projects such as counter tops, shelves, benches and end tables.

The basic procedure for slab cutting is to...

- Turn the log so that it lies as flat as possible on the mill, clamp it down, and cut boards of the desired thickness until reaching the center of the log.

- Then rotate the log 180 degrees, and finish milling from the other side.

- The widest boards at the center will be quarter sawn.

- The next board or two will be rift-sawn.

- And the first and outer boards will be flat-sawn.

This gives the woodworker a variety of patterns to work with.

Keep in mind, there may be some cupping issues with the flat-sawn boards especially if they are more than 10" wide.

A variation of slab cutting is to mill one side of the log to get a flat surface, and then turn the log 90 degrees for slabbing.

This is especially useful if the diameter of the log exceeds the maximum cutting width of the saw. It gives the woodworker the widest possible slabs with one straight and one natural edge.

For wider surfaces, such as a table, two pieces can be joined along their straight edges.

This can create stunning book-matched pieces where the grain and shape of one slab, is mirrored by the other slab.

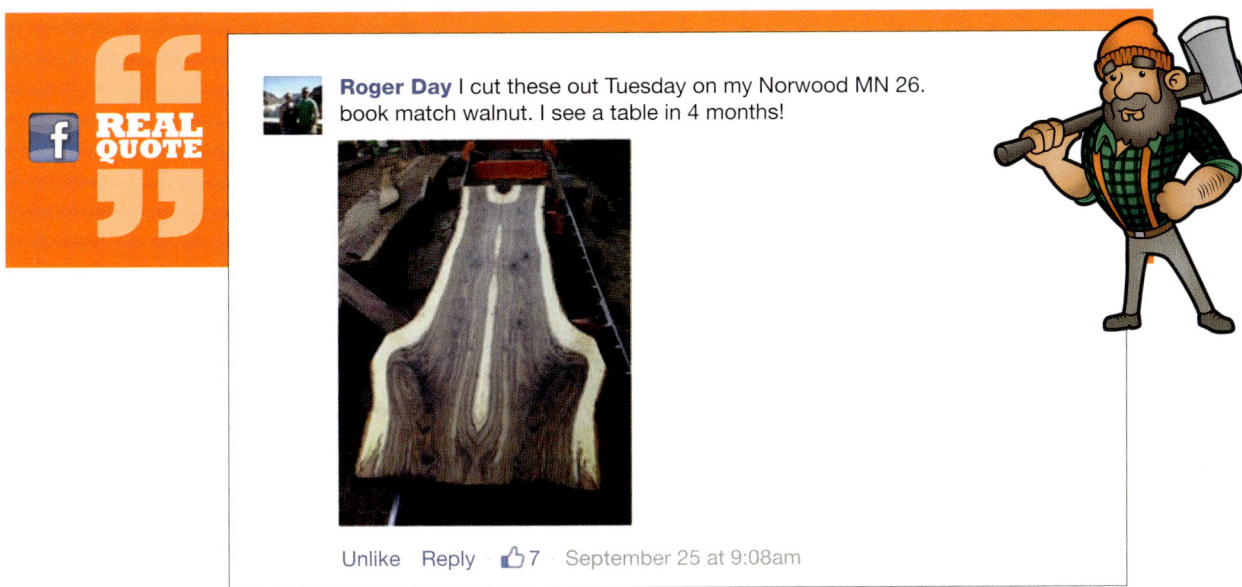

It is nearly impossible to get book-matched pieces unless you get them right off the mill.

The most efficient way to dry slabs is to put them in the same order in which they were originally arranged in the log, with 1" spacers between them.

They will be easy to move with a fork lift, and make it easier for the woodworker to match the grain for their projects.

This method is commonly called the "European" drying technique, though you may hear it called by other names as well.

Conclusion:

- Knowing these milling techniques is not only challenging and fun, it allows you to give your customer exactly what they want.

- Your customers will be thrilled because they know they will soon be working with wood that is not available at lumber yards at any price.

- You will have repeat customers, and a vibrant business, because very few sawyers are willing to go the extra mile to create specialty lumber.

f REAL QUOTE

Frank Vaillancourt My dad has been using same set up for years and years up north helped him for hours on end running it some of the best years of my life ! Beautiful set up can bring anywhere and get number one lumber you cant get at stores.

Unlike · Reply · 👍 1 · 13 hrs

Here are a few more hints to turning your sawing ability into a throng of happy customers singing your praises...

✓ Be sure to **keep in touch** with your customers.

✓ **Get photos of the end product**, so you can inspire other woodworkers to "think outside the box."

✓ If you have an unusual log, **make a few phone calls**. Often you'll hear, *"Don't touch that log until I can get there to tell you how I want it cut!"*

✓ This usually means you will **sell the lumber right away**, and for several times more than what you otherwise would have made from it.

✓ **Have fun, and enjoy creating unique lumber!** It's a win-win that will pay you back handsomely over and over again.

And that is how you maximize your sawing pattern potential!

Lumber Grading Basics

7

Even though you may never actually grade lumber yourself, it is important to understand the basics.

In general, the better the lumber grade, the higher the quality and the fewer the defects. And knowing the grade will help you (and potentially your customers) with lumber selection for projects.

Defects in your lumber may include pith, splits, knots, sticker stains, and worm holes. It's interesting to note that sap wood is not considered a defect, even though most people prefer to buy heart wood.

What's Up with Lumber Grading?

Every year, it seems to be more and more challenging to find consistently straight, smooth lumber from a commercial lumber yard. It's practically worthy of a celebration when you find several boards without splits, knots, or curvy edges.

It's a given that there must be a standard to set the quality of the lumber.

In fact, there are several standards, depending on the species of wood, and how it will be used. However, the standards are complicated and often confusing.

There are special courses and certifications for lumber grading. But if you are just a small business, why is lumber grading of any concern to you?

After all, you could just sell "mill run" lumber and let the buyer determine what he or she can use.

Here's Why You Should Care

An awareness of lumber grades can make you a better sawyer, and actually increase the value of your lumber.

In other words, you can leave all that "knotty" lumber to the commercial lumber yards, while YOU focus on creating straight and true lumber that is beautiful to behold AND to work with.

Lumber grading is the language of lumbermen (and women!) and clearly communicates what the buyer is getting.

If every log yielded perfect boards, lumber grading wouldn't be necessary. But nature has other ideas…and perhaps even a warped sense of humor.

In the perfectly imperfect scheme of things, logs have taper, crooks, forks, branches, and rot.

And that means a variety of lumber grades to choose from.

For example, a furniture manufacturer may require a higher quality, and is willing to pay a premium for it.

A cabinet shop that cuts the wood into small parts may be able to cut around the defects, and lower its manufacturing cost by buying a lower grade of lumber.

The poorest grade lumber might go to a pallet manufacturer to recover a little more income from the board.

Knowing which boards to send each buyer, not only helps the bottom line, but may keep you out of potential problems with disgruntled customers as well.

In the simplest terms, hardwood lumber grades describe how much clear wood can be cut out of a board.

Defects can be identified as anything reducing the quality of the board, either structurally or aesthetically, including...

✓ **Splits**

✓ **Knots**

Round knot

Spike knot

✓ **Bark Inclusions**

✓ **Pitch pockets**

✓ **Rot**

✓ **Stains from stickers**

✓ **Fungus**

✓ **Wane**

Making the Grade

It is fascinating to watch an experienced lumber grader at work.

With boards coming down the line one after another, the lumber grader glances at each board, flips it over to check the other side, and then routes it to the correct conveyer, all in less than TWO seconds.

FAS (Firsts & Seconds) is the highest grade, though it does allow for some defects.

FAS lumber gives the clearest wood, and is suited for quality furniture.

FAS boards must be at least 6" wide by 8' long.

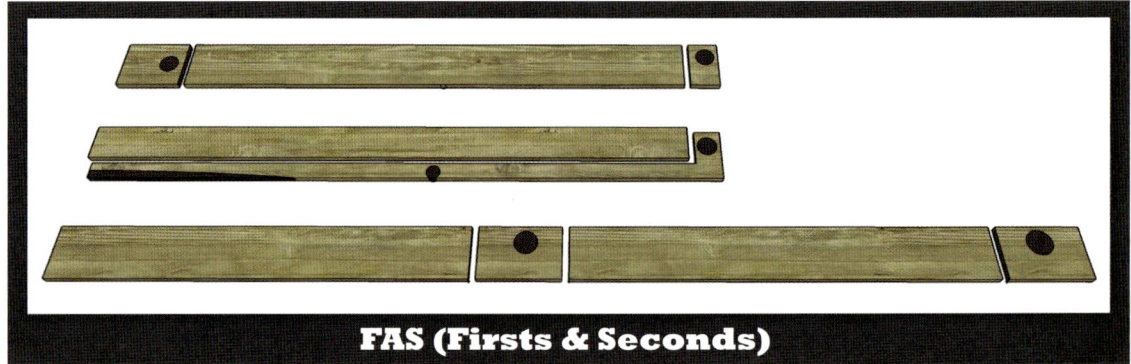

FAS (Firsts & Seconds)

In comparison, 83% of the **worst** face must yield clear boards at least 3" wide by 7' long, or 4" wide by 5' long.

FAS lumber is the most valuable, so knowing how to get the most out of a log can make a big difference to your profitability.

Number 1 Common is often referred to as "cabinet grade" lumber.

This is because it is often used for that purpose. As a rule of thumb, 2/3 of the wood has to be clear to make boards at least 3" wide and 4' long.

To qualify as Number 1 Common, both faces must meet or exceed this standard.

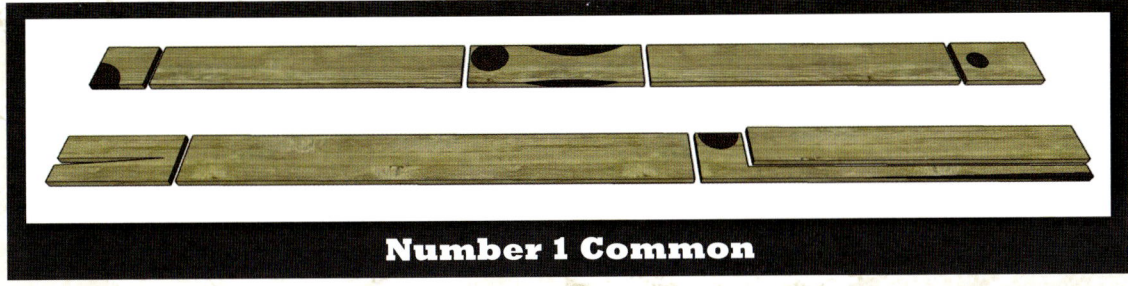

Number 1 Common

Number 2A Common is called "economy grade" because it is the least expensive.

It is commonly used for small furniture parts, or for pieces that are out of sight.

At least 50% of the wood must be clear to make boards at least 3" wide and 2' long.

Number 2A is graded from its poorest side, so even if the good side is a higher grade, the board is still Number 2A common.

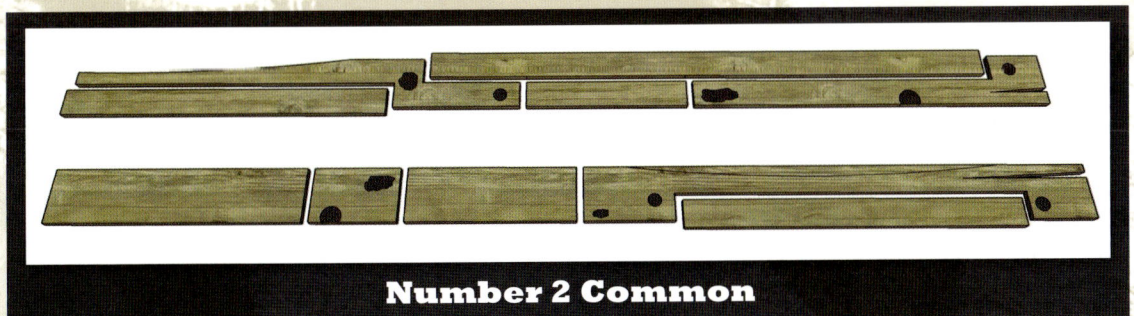

Number 2 Common

Gaining the Advantage with Grading

Here is how you can use grading rules to your advantage.

✓ Open the log (first slabbing cut) on the side of the log that looks the clearest.

✓ Then cut the other three sides to get a square cant.

✓ From there, cut the best face until there is enough defect to drop it down a grade.

✓ Then turn the cant to the next best face and do the same.

In theory, this puts most of the defect into the fewest boards.

This simple technique can increase the value of your lumber by as much as 10%, without costing you a penny!

Experienced edger operators can often trim defects off the edges or ends of boards to get enough clear wood to bump the board up a grade.

The increase in value of the remaining wood more than makes up for the loss in lumber volume.

Experienced sawyers also know that the lowest quality wood is near the center of the log. This is where the branches were when the tree was small.

Leveling tapered logs so that the center of the log is parallel to the track keeps this center defect in as few boards as possible.

What About if You're Building Bigger?

Softwood lumber grading rules in America are established by the U.S. Department of Commerce.

The rules are similar in concept, but are oriented toward **construction** lumber.

As such, it is **graded for its structural properties**.

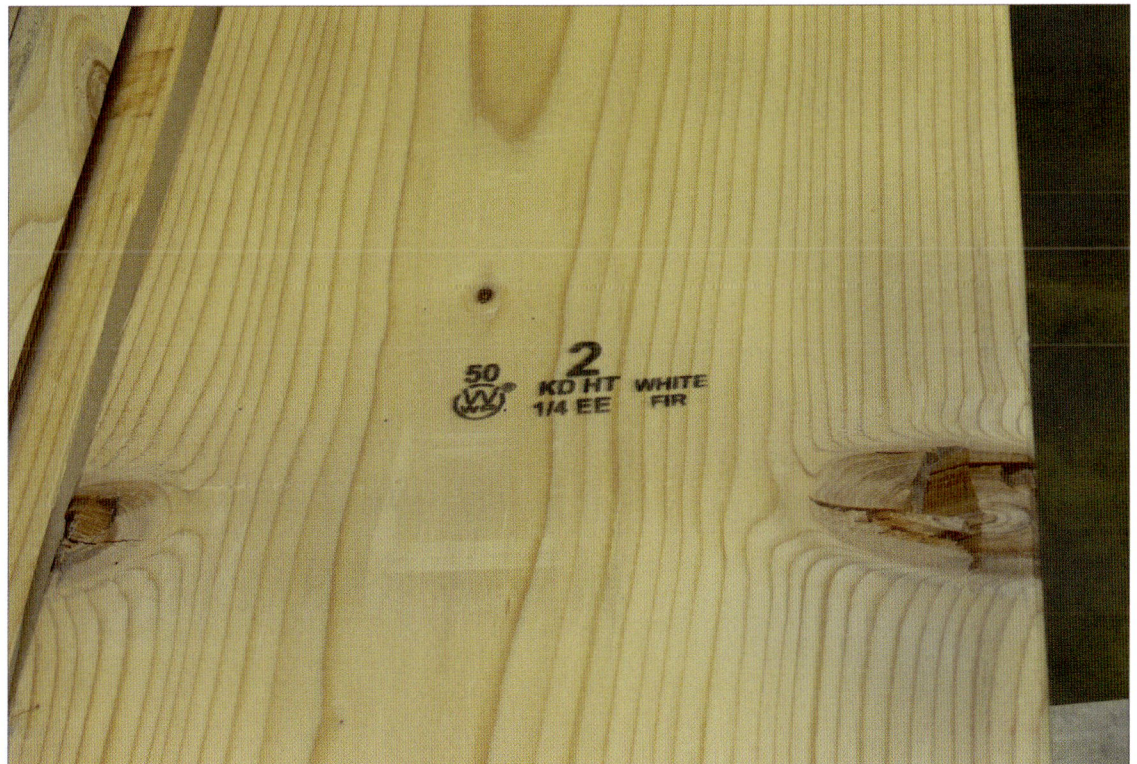

The grade assigned to a board is based on the location and size of defects over the entire length.

Grades themselves are based on location, size, and placement of knots, slope of grain, manufacturing defects, wane, warp, and species.

Within each grade, there is a range of values allowed. The idea is to be sure the wood is up to the job of bearing the load placed on it.

Nearly all building codes require graded, stamped lumber, and only a certified grader can apply the stamp.

Even if your Douglas fir stud has perfectly straight grain and is free of knots, without that stamp by a certified grader, it may not be used if building codes require certified lumber.

The worst case scenario (and it HAS happened!) is that a completed building will be torn down because certified lumber was not used.

This is why you and your customers need to be aware of the codes in your area before you ever start making sawdust.

There is a great deal of information about lumber grading on the Internet, and courses are offered by organizations such as the National Hardwood Lumber Association and the Softwood Lumber Board.

Certification courses can take up to six weeks to complete, but there are also "short courses" available that are intended to provide basic information on grading standards.

"Making the grade" can seem a little overwhelming at first, but by arming yourself with some basic knowledge, it will soon become second nature to consider your lumber grades when you are milling logs.

50 Smart Tips & Tricks for Sawyers

8

1. It is generally easier to mill from the small end of a tapered log. That helps you line up your cuts better.

2. If you are just starting out, draw out your cutting pattern on the end of the log. It will help you visualize what you are doing.

3. If you are milling a log that pushes the capacity of your mill, turn it so that you start cutting from the big end. That makes it easier to see whether you'll need to trim it with a chain saw before you start milling.

4. Load logs with a bell-shaped flair so that as much of the flair as possible hangs over the cross bunk. That makes leveling the log easier and, in many cases, you can do without leveling the log.

5. Use toe boards, shims, or a jack to level logs with taper. The idea is to have the centerline of the log parallel to the track.

6. When setting up a mill, make sure it is level lengthwise and crosswise. This keeps the carriage from moving on its own, and makes it easier to square up the log.

7. For best quality, the first cut, or the "opening face", should be on the best (straightest and clearest) side of the log.

8. If the log has a lot of flair or taper, you might want to make several light cuts so you don't have to handle heavy slabs.

9. Keep yourself in shape, too. Safety gear should include eye and hearing protection, steel-toe boots, and gloves. Drink plenty of fluids when it is hot, and stop when you are fatigued. That last log will wait.

10. Dirt on the log dulls the blade quickly! If possible, turn the log so that dirt is on the side of the log that the blade exits. This will save you the time of cleaning up the log. Use a hatchet, or even the chainsaw to remove the dirt from the side of the log that the blade enters.

11. The first turn (if turning the log 90 degrees) is the most critical, in terms of squaring up the log. Use a plumb level to check the flat side (from the first cut). This makes sure that the log will be cut square.

12. Some logs lie flatter on the mill or are easier to clamp down if you turn them 180 degrees after the first opening cut, so that the third face cut is the 90 degree squaring cut. This is especially true if there is a bump on the log that would rest on a cross-bunk.

13. Logs with a bend to them can be a challenge to line up and clamp down. The easiest procedure is to make the opening cut with the ends of the log bowed upwards. Then mill normally.

14. Do your best to keep the center of the growth rings centered in the cant as you mill. This minimizes any bowing in the boards as they dry.

15. If you are cutting 1" thick boards, do not remove the boards when you get to the bottom of the cant. The weight of the cut boards will help keep it flat.

16. Never try to pull the carriage backwards when the blade is spinning. It is almost guaranteed to come off the bandwheels.

17. If you need to back the blade out of a cut, tap plastic wedges (or you can make a wooden wedge, in a pinch) into the end of the cut to open up the kerf and make it easier to pull the blade out.

18. It is almost certain that you will eventually cut low enough to hit a clamp or log stop. Don't be too hard on yourself. Just chalk it up to experience, put on a fresh blade and keep on milling!

19. Pitch build-up on the blade can be a real problem with softwoods, but even hardwoods can have pitch build-up at certain times of the year. Everyone has his or her own recipe. If you add ¼ cup of PineSol and 1/8 cup of Simple Green to each tank of water and set the drip to a light, steady stream, your blade will stay clean. Some people also put in a little dishwashing detergent.

20. If the log has a knot, branch, flair, or other feature that might get in your way, cut it off while the log is still on the ground. According to *Murphy's Law*, if it can get in the way, it will.

21. If you are cutting crotch wood, turn the crotch so you cut through it sideways (crotch turned horizontally). You might get some beautiful feathered grain where the two pieces come together.

22. Short logs (4-feet or under) can be challenging, but rewarding. If the log stops and cross-bunks are too far apart, bridge across the cross-bunks with a good board, so that one clamp will hold it. Then use a second board to bridge across the log stops.

This is a sacrifice board. That is, you will cut this one as you cut the short board, so use one of low quality for this. Sometimes you can get some amazing boards this way. If you plan on milling short often, consider adding an extra cross-bunk kit and extra set of log clamping station receivers.

23. The blade is designed to turn at the optimum speed with the engine at full throttle. If you push hard enough to lug down the engine, or cut at partial throttle, you risk getting wavy cuts.

24. You know it is time to change a blade when:

a) It just won't cut straight.
b) You can feel it get easier to push the carriage when you reach the end of the cut.
c) The engine lugs down at normal feed rates.
d) You hit any metal with it.
e) The blade leaves a rough finish on the log.

25. Band saw mills can cut perfectly straight lumber. Here are a few things to look at if you are getting wavy cuts:

a) The blade is dull. You may have hit some dirt in the bark.
b) The blade teeth are not properly set.
c) You are pushing too fast or too slow – listen to the engine.
d) The blade is not tracking correctly on the bandwheels.
e) There is not enough tension on the blade.
f) Blade guides are not holding the blade perfectly parallel to the track.
g) The drive belt is slipping.
h) The engine is not running at full throttle.
i) There is pitch build-up on the blade.
j) There is a large knot in the log (slow way down when sawing through knots).
k) Some woods, such as pecan, hickory, and spruce have a grain that naturally tries to deflect the blade. You need a sharp blade and more tension for these species.

26. When loading or turning logs, make sure the log stops are up high enough to keep the log from rolling off the mill.

27. Winching logs up a ramp onto the mill is easy if you run the winch line over the top of the log, then under the log and back to the log deck. This doubles the pulling force of the winch and rolls the log right up. This technique is called "parbuckling" the log.

28. Many large trees have limbs big enough to cut on a sawmill, but these are usually trouble. The stress in limb wood usually causes it to warp either while milling or as the wood dries.

29. All logs have stress in them. If a board curls up as you cut it, turn the cant 180 degrees to equalize out the stress before you make the next cut. If the log bows sideways, turn the log 90 degrees before making the next cut.

30. Saw a few consistent thicknesses. This will make the boards much easier to stack for drying.

31. Never "hot wire" around safety switches on a sawmill or remove guards. They are there for your protection.

32. If you anticipate spectators, flag off the "danger zone". This includes the area where the sawdust exits the mill to about fifty feet away from the mill. Chunks of wood can fly a surprising distance!

33. Plan ahead for slab and sawdust removal. If you have a front end loader available, put two large slabs down crosswise to hold the rest of the slabs and edgings off the ground so the loader can get under them easily to move them.

34. The less you handle boards, the better! If possible, off-bear the boards right into a waiting a truck or trailer so that they can be transported directly to where they will be air dried.

35. The easiest way to edge lumber on the sawmill is to mill the cant down to 5" to 6" thick. Then use the cant as backing to support the boards to be edged. You can edge three or four boards at a time this way.

36. Cut 6" by 6" blocking out of your worst logs so that you have a way to hold piles of lumber off the ground as it air dries. You'll need one at least every 24" for 1" thick boards.

37. As you edge your lumber on the mill, be sure to cut plenty of stickers to use as spacers between the layers of boards as they dry. This is a good use for low quality lumber.

38. If you don't have a good cant hook (or peavey, if you prefer), get one. It will become like an extension to your arm. Two are even better – one with a 4' handle, and one with a 5' handle.

39. A chain saw is an important tool. Keep it sharp and in good running condition. Wear sawing chaps, and face and hearing protection when you use it, and be sure of your footing before you start to cut. Use the chain brake any time that you are not cutting but the saw is running. Trimming logs with a chain saw can be the most dangerous part of sawmilling.

40. Keep a special "Sawmill Toolbox" with the most commonly used tools, so that they're always handy.

41. When you flip a cant 180 degrees, the next cut should be perfectly square. If the board has a side-to-side taper, the blade is not parallel to the crossbunks. Check the blade guides, and adjust them, if necessary. If you still have a problem getting square cuts, adjust the low side of the carriage up ½ the amount the board taper, and re-set the height gauge.

42. a) If your mill uses roller guides, check the pressure of the blade against the guides, and make sure they turn easily. A flat spot on the guide is a sure sign of a bad bearing.

b) If your mill uses ceramic guides, check them periodically to make sure that they are centered on the blade with a slight gap (no more than a sheet of paper) above and below between the ceramic blocks and the blade. Check for chipped blocks. You can usually turn them over and keep using them, but it is a good idea to have a few extras in your toolbox.

43. When you change blades, check the tracking (where the blade rides on the bandwheels) with the new blade at operating tension. If necessary, adjust the tracking so that the body of the blade is centered on the bandwheel. Blades can stretch and sharpening removes some of the width of the blade, so tracking may vary from one blade to another.

44. Unless your bandwheels use sealed bearings, give them a shot of grease each time you change blades.

45. The sawmill operates in a very dusty environment. Clean the air filter every 10 hours, and replace it regularly. The fuel filter also needs regular changing. Sawdust gets everywhere, even in the fuel tank.

46. Always loosen the blade at the end of the day so it doesn't take a curved set that can cause vibration when you mill with it.

47. How about building a log deck for your first project? It will make loading the mill faster, easier, and safer.

48. A mill shed is another great project and protects your investment from the elements.

49. To keep the wood from cracking on the ends, apply a heavy coat of latex paint or an end-sealant such as AnchorSeal to the ends of the logs or boards.

50. Stack and sticker boards for air drying as soon as possible after milling. They should be stacked where there is good air circulation through the stack and covered to protect the stack from rain. Extra weight on the top will help keep them flat as they dry.

In Conclusion...

We sincerely hope you have found value throughout these pages.

By now, it is likely your eyes have been opened to the vast scope of possibilities ahead of you with portable sawmill ownership.

And it's true, that milling is somewhat addictive!

It's been our experience, that once you take the first step, you'll be just as connected to what you can do with your milling as this happy sawmill owner...

The fact is, portable sawmills are literally changing lives in multiple ways…

With the opportunity to build a home AND a business...

"When I move into my house, it's going to be paid for on account of this sawmill. It's the best thing I've ever done." — Lonnie Hunt

Hear how Lonnie has built a business and a house with his Norwood portable sawmill.

www.NorwoodSawmills.com

Once you get sawdust in your veins, you'll see potential everywhere...

David Boyt ▸ **Norwood Portable Sawmills**

November 4, 2014 · 🌐

Another "trash to treasure" adventure. This honeylocust was bound for a firewood pile before I rescued it. By removing the ceramic guides and cutting very carefully, I was able to cut slabs nearly 32" wide.

And before you know it, you'll be sharing photos of your handiwork too!

Brad Mills ▶ **Norwood Portable Sawmills** ·

December 19, 2014

The one hr. Christmas bench, Makes a great gift. Easy and fast with my Norwood HD 36 and a chain saw.

Like Comment Share

👍 9 people like this.   Top comments ▾

🔖 71 shares

Billy Welch Zimmerman Nice
Like Reply 1   December 19, 2014 at 8:35pm

Dawn M O Dell Love the red in the wood. thats pretty nice. Do you like it?
Like Reply 1   December 19, 2014 at 5:45pm

N **Norwood Portable Sawmills** Great idea Brad!! Looks great.
Like Reply   December 19, 2014 at 4:50pm

 Monika Marcinko ▶ **Norwood Portable Sawmills**

July 18, 2014 · 🌐

Just like Curtis Duffer you can make your dreams come true!

Like Comment Share

👍 9 people like this.

🔖 21 shares

Jeffrey Beyer Gorgeous!
Like Reply July 27, 2014 at 1:19pm

A legion of raving fans agree...the investment in their portable sawmills has been well worth it...

REAL QUOTE

 Tom Nelson After 15 years still love my Lumbermate.... Especially when I install a new blade!!
Like· Reply · 👍 4 · June 23, 2013 at 10:47pm

 Mark St Onge I purchased a mx34 w/ the 23hp this spring, Love it. I've been sawing cherry and red oak, it is so smooth, cuts like butter, plenty of power. My problem is that I would rather saw logs than go to work! I love the electric start, I turn it off when rolling and re-log dogging the cant. A little hint, change blades often, when they start getting "funky" change them, for $7 a blade to sharpen, it's not worth dulling them to a point of no return. make sure you join the Norwood Forum for lots of great tips and conversation, Mark
Like· Reply · 👍 3 · June 23, 2013 at 10:40pm

 Brigitte LeGresley We got the LumberMate LM29 Series with the Honda 13hp engine and it's great on gas, it works great and it runs really smooth. Really happy that we went with Norwood. 😬
Like· Reply · 👍 4 · June 23, 2013 at 10:09pm

 Charlie Brunner I purchased a ML26 a year and a half ago and was really pleased with the quality and ease of use. I bought the 13hp engine upgrade and a 4 foot bed extension. Have not had any problems at all with the mill and the Honda engine normally starts on the first pull. Check out the barn myself, my son and grandson built with our mill in Norwoods 2012 Photo Challenge
Like· Reply · 👍 2 · June 23, 2013 at 10:30pm

 Scott Shaeffer We got a variety of add-ons for our LumberMate Pro and only one of them didn't really suit our needs and even after procrastinating the return for a month, Norwood still took it back and credited our account. So that makes me feel good about trying different add-ons knowing I can send them back if I don't like them.
Like· Reply · June 26, 2013 at 10:34am

 David Boyt A lot depends on what you'll be cutting. I've got the MX34, trailer package, 2-ft extension, loading ramp and winch--and I can't imagine working without them. Get the biggest engine option for the mill, an extra 20 blades, and a couple of good cant hooks. Mill itself runs great. Norwood has put a lot of thought into their mills.
Like· Reply · 👍 1 · June 24, 2013 at 10:00am

All Around The World Dreams Are Being Fulfilled

From North America...

To Europe...

To Asia...

To Africa...

When Peter Dale had his vision for the first Norwood Portable Sawmill, he had no idea how vast the impact would be.

- *All around the world, dreams are being fulfilled and lives changed.*

- *Communities, families, and friends are joined together in entirely new ways.*

- *Memories are created, legacies fulfilled, and businesses born.*

If you're still deciding if a portable sawmill is for you, and the desire to get busy cutting logs just won't go away, consider the words of the great Mark Twain…

> *"Twenty years from now you will be more disappointed by the things that you didn't do than by the ones you did do. So throw off the bowlines. Sail away from the safe harbor. Catch the trade winds in your sails. Explore. Dream. Discover."*
> — Mark Twain

Life is far too short to put your dreams on the back burner. Consider for a moment what doors can open for you as you ***"explore, dream, and discover"*** what is possible for YOU when you become the proud owner of your own portable sawmill.

And please don't hesitate to get in touch if you have any questions, or would like to know more about how portable sawmill ownership can become a reality for you, no matter where you may be in the world.

NorwoodSawmills.com
info@NorwoodSawmills.com
1-800-567-0404 (within North America)
+1-705-689-2800 (outside North America)

To your milling success,
The Norwood Team

Appendix:
Sawmill Terminology & Definitions

Air Dry: Wood that has been dried by allowing air to circulate through the boards. Typically, this ranges between 12% and 14% moisture content.

Band Sawmill: Sawmill that mills lumber by use of a band saw blade.

Bandwheel: Wheel on a band sawmill that turns the band saw blade.

Blade Lubricant: Liquid applied to a band saw blade to minimize friction between the blade and the wood. Often includes a solvent to minimize pitch build-up on the blade.

Blade Tension: Tension, or "tightness" of the band saw blade, measured in pounds.

Blocking: Wood cut 3" by 3" or larger, usually for holding material off the ground.

Blue Stain: Coloration of the wood, usually due to fungus. May also be an indication of ferrous metal embedded in the wood.

Board Foot: A measure of wood: Volume equivalent to 12" long, 12" wide, and 1" thick (144 cubic inches).

Bow: Gradual bend, or curve in a log. May also refer to a sideways curve in a board.

Butt Log: The first, or bottom log from a tree. Usually contains the highest quality lumber.

Cant: A log that has been squared off by sawing.

Cant Hook: Blunt-nosed tool for rolling or rotating a log or cant.

Check: Crack in a log or board, usually due to drying.

Clamp: Device that applies pressure to hold the log in place while milling.

Crook: Sharp bend in a log.

Crossbunk: Crosspieces on the bed of the sawmill that support the log.

Crotch: "Y" or "U" shaped fork in a log, each side of roughly equal size.

Cup: Curling of a board width-wise. Usually caused by stress while drying.

Deck: Structure that holds logs off the ground so that they can be lifted or rolled onto the sawmill.

Dog (n): May refer to the log stop or the clamp.

Dog (v): To set the sawmill clamps into a log.

Doyle Scale: Log scale that estimates the amount of lumber that can be cut from a log. Usually used with hardwood logs, it underestimates the volume of logs under 20" diameter.

Dunnage: Low-quality lumber, usually for pallets or blocking.

Edging: To cut the bark of the edge of a board so that it has a straight, clean edge down its length.

End Check: Cracks that form in the end of a log or board, usually perpendicular to the growth rings. Uneven drying that occurs due to faster moisture movement out the ends of the logs or boards than through the sides causes the cracks.

End Sealer: Material (usually a wax) applied to the ends of logs and/or boards to slow down moisture movement and reduce end checks.

Flat Sawn: Saw cut parallel to the growth rings.

Flitch *(n)*: Board with natural ("live") edges on both sides.

Flitch *(v)*: To cut a log straight through so that all boards have natural ("live") edges.

Green: Lumber fresh off the sawmill, usually with moisture content of 50% or more. May also refer to a recently cut log.

Gullet: Cutout area between teeth that carries the sawdust out of the cut.

Hardwood: Technically, these are classified as *angiosperms* (covered seeds). Generally they have broad leaves and are deciduous (lose their leaves in the winter) but there are exceptions. The wood is generally harder than most softwoods, but there are exceptions to this, too.

Heartwood: The inner wood of a tree or log. This is usually darker than the outer sapwood.

Hook Angle: Angle at which the tooth of the blade meets the wood – usually between 10 degrees for soft woods to 4 degrees for dense, hard woods.

Hydraulic Sawmill: A sawmill with hydraulic assist for log handling, carriage feed, and blade height adjustment.

International ¼" Scale: A log scale developed to accurately predict the amount of wood in a log, allowing for a ¼" saw kerf.

Kerf: Thickness of the sawmill cut in the wood; usually about 1/8" for band sawmills and ¼" to 5/16" for circle mills.

Kiln: Facility for drying lumber to 6% to 8% moisture content, usually by a combination of heat, dehumidification, and controlled airflow.

Kiln Dry: Wood that has been dried to 6% to 8% moisture content.

Live Edge: Edge of a board with its natural shape.

Log Deck: Structure that holds logs to be milled off the ground.

Log Stop: Vertical member of a sawmill that supports the log when the clamp is applied.

Manual Sawmill: Sawmill that has no power-assist features.

Nominal Size: Named dimensions of a log, which may not correspond to the actual size, e.g. a nominal 2x4 is actually 1-1/2" by 3-1/2".

Offbear: To remove slabs and lumber from the sawmill.

Parbuckle: Technique for winching logs up a ramp, by running the winch line around the top of the log and back to the winch so that it rolls the log.

Peavey: Pointed-nosed tool for rolling or rotating a log or cant.

Pitch (a): Distance between the teeth of a saw blade.

Pitch (b): Resin or sap in a log.

Pith: The center of the growth rings.

Portable Sawmill: Sawmill designed to be movable; usually mounted on axles for easy towing.

Quarter Sawn: Wood cut perpendicular to the growth rings.

Reaction Wood: Wood put on as the tree grows as a response to leaning or other physical stress. May cause a board or cant to bend as it is cut, resulting in boards of uneven thickness.

Rift Sawn: Wood with a growth ring angle between 45% and 75% to the face of the board.

Ring Check (or Ring Shake): Cracks in a log that follow the growth rings.

Sapwood: The outer part of a tree or log, usually distinctly lighter in color than the inner heartwood.

Scale Stick: Measuring stick with markings that indicate the estimated volume of a log, based on the length and diameter.

Set: Amount by which the tooth is bent to allow it to make a slightly wider cut than the thickness of the blade.

Setworks: Mechanism for moving the log or saw blade to mill boards of the desired width.

Slab: The rounded outer portion cut from a log.

Softwood: Technically, these are classified as *gymnosperms* (naked seeds). Generally they have needles instead of leaves and are evergreen but there are exceptions. The wood is generally softer than most hardwoods, but there are exceptions to this, too.

Spalting: Discoloration of wood due to fungus. In some light-colored woods it can create attractive patterns.

Sticker: Square spacers placed between layers of boards to allow air circulation through the stack for air-drying.

Taper: Difference in diameter of the ends of a log.

Toe Board: Device on a sawmill that levels a log with taper. May have a roller to allow easy positioning of the log on the mill.

Tracking: Angle of a bandwheel to the blade. Usually set so that the blade is centered.

Widow Maker: Usually refers to a dead branch in a tree, but can apply to any hazardous situation that has a potentially fatal consequence.

Testimonials

"I made the curio cabinet as a wedding present for my son and his wife. I harvested the silver maple on land owned by my family since 1895. Although it cannot be seen in the photo, I built the drawer bottom from red oak I harvested off family land in 2002 that was 107 years old. I include a piece from that red oak in every piece of furniture I make because it sprouted in 1895, the year my great-grandfather purchased the land.

I ordered my Norwood LumberMate to mill enough lumber to construct a 24' by 51' shed, but fell in love with milling. So, after building the shed, I continued to mill enough for a hunting cabin, several hardwood floors and then furniture. My milled inventory includes enough white ash flooring, sugar maple baseboard and casing, and furniture cherry for my other two children's homes.

My son and his wife take great pride when showing their new home because Billy helped harvest, skid, mill, plane, shape, sand, stain and install the flooring and casing in his home. I managed to surprise him with the curio cabinet even though he milled the boards with me on the LumberMate. I should note I am not a professional logger, miller or woodworker. I escape to my LumberMate whenever I can after leaving work as a circuit-court judge."

— William M. Atkinson, MI

> *"Just wanted to tell you guys that we would be kind of lost without our mill. I bought this mill from you a few years ago and have thought maybe I might sell it a couple times but I didn't. We have built camps, barns, sheds, sawed wood for projects, plus sawed a lot for other people. I'd be lost without it."*
>
> — Bruce Blodgett, NH

"We want to thank you for all your help in making our lives go a lot easier in building our house. Keep up the good work in manufacturing your wonderful product."

— David and Dana Martin, NE

"I cannot say thank you enough to everyone at Norwood. Having dealt with, taught and worked in customer service all my life, you, your company, its employees have it right.

I cannot imagine anyone buying another company's product. I wish I could shout that to anyone looking for a mill. "You are crazy to buy anything else!""

— Kevin Kesick, NY

Notes

Notes

Notes

Notes